CW00428727

MEMORIE
OF
YORK

TRUE NORTH BOOKS

DEAN CLOUGH
HALIFAX
WEST YORKSHIRE
HX3 5AX
TEL 01422 344344

ACKNOWLEDGMENTS

THE PUBLISHERS WOULD LIKE TO THANK THE FOLLOWING COMPANIES FOR SUPPORTING THE PRODUCTION OF THIS BOOK

BARNITTS LTD.

R. S. COCKERILL (YORK) LTD.

DERWENT COACHWORKS

GARBUTT AND ELLIOTT

LONDONS

MULBERRY HALL

NESTLÉ U.K. LTD.

DICK REID

RIDINGS CONSTRUCTION CO.

J.H. SHOUKSMOUTH & SONS LTD.

TURNBULLS (YORK) LTD.

YACHT SERVICES LTD. (NABURN MARINA)

YORK AUTOLECTRICS LTD.

THANKS ARE DUE TO THE FOLLOWING PEOPLE AND ORGANISATIONS FOR HELPING WITH THE SUPPLY OF PHOTOGRAPHS:

CITY OF YORK COUNCIL - LEISURE SERVICES (YORK LIBRARY)

JOE MURPHY

DAVID BATTERS

THE NATIONAL RAILWAY MUSEUM

WALTER SCOTT PHOTOGRAPHERS

WOOD VISUAL COMMUNICATIONS

First published in Great Britain by True North Books
Dean Clough
Halifax HX3 5AX
1998

© TRUE NORTH HOLDINGS

ISBN 1 900 463 66 0

Introduction

York's attractive open market in the 1960s.

Welcome to *Memories of York*, a look back on some of the places, events and people in the city which have shaped our lives over a period of around half a century. The following pages are brought to life by the selection of images from the not-too-distant past, chosen according to their ability to rekindle memories of days gone by and show how people used to shop, work and play in the city where they grew up. Modern image reproduction techniques have enabled us to present these pictures in a way rarely seen before, and the lively design and informative text has attempted to set the book apart from some of the other works available. The chosen period covered here is one which contains events within the memory of a large number of people in York - this is not a book about crino-lines or bowler-hats! Neither is *Memories of York* a work of local history in the normal sense of the words. It has far more to do with entertainment than serious study, but we hope you will agree it is none the worse for that.

Many local companies and organisations have allowed us to study their archives and include their history - and fascinating reading it makes too. The present-day guardians of the companies concerned are proud of their products, the achievements of their people and the hard work of their forefathers whose efforts created these long established firms in the first place. We are pleased to play our part by making it possible for them to share their history with a wider audience.

We have tried to create an interesting blend of photographs capable of informing and entertaining the reader. There are scores of images of local people in the book, deliberately chosen because many of them will have survived to the present time. We hope that these photographs will bring back happy memories for the people concerned and their families.

When we began compiling *Memories of York* several months ago we anticipated that the task would be a pleasurable one, but our expectations were greatly surpassed. The quality of the photographs we have been privileged to use has been superb. There is a growing appetite for all things 'nostalgic' and we are pleased to

have played a small part in swelling the number of images and associated information available to the growing number of nostalgia enthusiasts.

There is much talk in modern times about the regener-ation of the local economy, the influx of new industries and the challenge of attracting new enterprise from other regions to the area. And quite right too. We could, however, make the mistake of thinking that the changes are all happening *now*, but the reality is that there have always been major developments going on York. 'Change' is relentless and the photographs on the pages of the book serve to remind us of a mere selection of them. York has been fortunate in retaining most of its character and fine historic buildings over the last century, unlike many other other northern towns and cities.

Some of the images fall outside the qualification we describe as 'within living memory', but most of these will be familiar to us, either because they concern an event described to us by a close relative, or they feature monuments such as the businesses or buildings we simply felt compelled to include. Whatever the view taken on the boundaries which separate 'history', 'nostalgia' and the present time, we should all invest a few moments occasionally to reflect on the past and the events which made the City what it is today. *Memories of York* has been a pleasure to compile, we sincerely hope you enjoy reading it. Happy memories!

Phil Holland

COVER DESIGN/PHOTOGRAPHS COMPILED BY MARK SMITH

CAPTIONS COMPILED BY PHIL HOLLAND

TEXT PAGES DESIGNED BY MANDY WALKER/NICKY BRIGHTON

LOCAL BUSINESS CONTENT ORGANISED BY STUART GLENHOLMES

Contents

Right: We can only guess at the thoughts going through the minds of the people on this horse and cart as it rescues them from their water-logged homes. The picture dates from 1947, but it could have been taken on dozens of other occasions during the period covered by this book. The street shown here is Walker Street, a mainly residential area with only few business premises. The area was always one of the first to suffer when the Ouse rose over its banks, and it was not until the early 1990s that really effective flood control was introduced to keep the water at bay.

Around the walls

A proud royal occasion in York was recorded by this photograph which was taken on June 28th 1971. The immaculately-turned-out horsemen of the Household Cavalry are shown entering the city through Micklegate Bar, the traditional entrance used by the reigning Monarch on visits to York. Her Majesty Queen Elizabeth II had arrived at the Ruforth airfield at 11.30am on the morning of the visit, accompanied by His Royal Highness The Duke of Edinburgh. They went on by car to the racecourse at the Knavesmire where they were met by the Lord Mayor of York Alderman Richard Scruton and the Lady Mayoress. There followed a full 21 gun salute, the whole proceedings watched by over 1000 local schoolchildren as well as thousands of excited onlookers, ordinary York residents eager to demonstrate their support for their queen. The royal party went on to eat a grand lunch at the Georgian Assembly Rooms, accompanied by local worthies and the mayors of many neighbouring towns. A short walk to the Museum Gardens led to a further engagement attended by her Majesty and 2000 invited guests. The Queen chatted in a relaxed manner and one guest remembered how the warmth of her smile lit up the whole of the city on the day. A low-level fly-past of R.A.F fighter planes had everyone looking skywards, completing a day that would endure in the memories of those in attendance for the rest of their lives.

Above: This view looks towards Bootham Bar from Petergate. A sign on the left indicates the location of the Bootham Bar Café. Another café across the road was run by G.T Neesams and incorporated a confectioners. The Little family ran a private bed and breakfast establishment at number 98, as well as a 'skin rug making' business next door at number 97. The York Arms Hotel is featured in the picture, known for selling Hewitt's Grimsby Ales. Bootham Bar is the only one of the four York Bars which stands on the original site of the Porta Principalis Dextra, or right gateway, located here from the time of the Romans.

Right: An almost 'postcard' composition for this picture taken in 1955, showing the city walls and immaculate embankment. The imposing outline of the Minster can be seen in the distance, beyond Lendal Bridge and Museum Street. Rougier Street is just in view on the right of the picture. The Minster itself is York's most famous landmark and can lay claim to being the largest Mediaeval Gothic cathedral in England. To the modern observer it is a remarkable structure, made all the more so when one considers that it was constructed without the use of mechanical cranes, tools, transportation methods and other equipment that builders take for granted today.

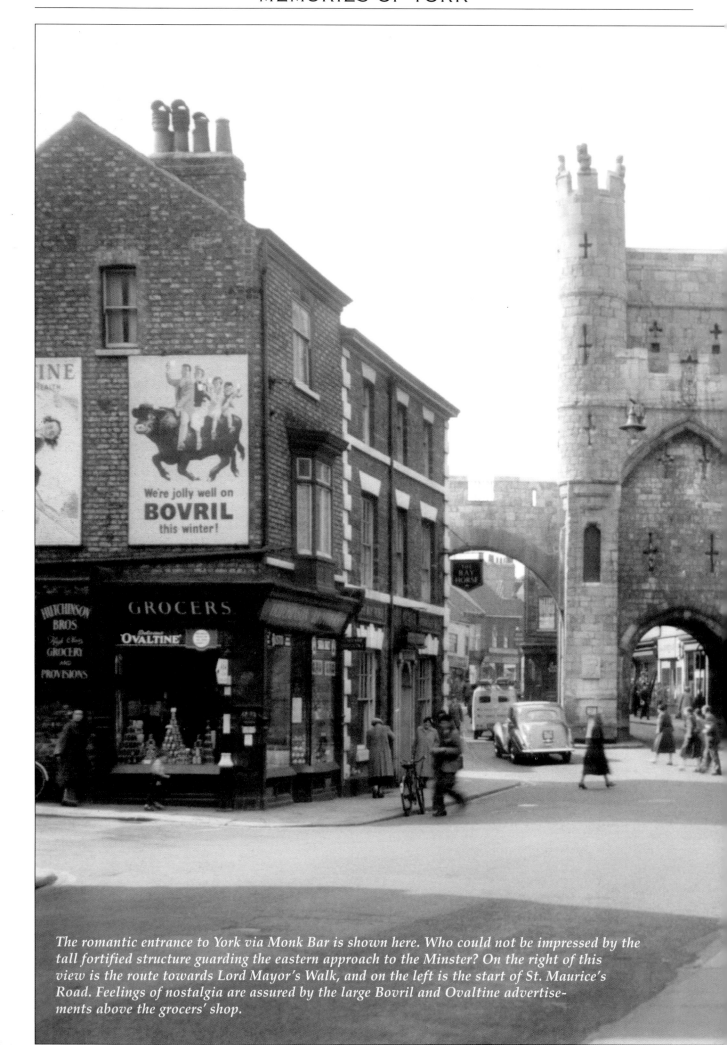

The romantic entrance to York via Monk Bar is shown here. Who could not be impressed by the tall fortified structure guarding the eastern approach to the Minster? On the right of this view is the route towards Lord Mayor's Walk, and on the left is the start of St. Maurice's Road. Feelings of nostalgia are assured by the large Bovril and Ovaltine advertisements above the grocers' shop.

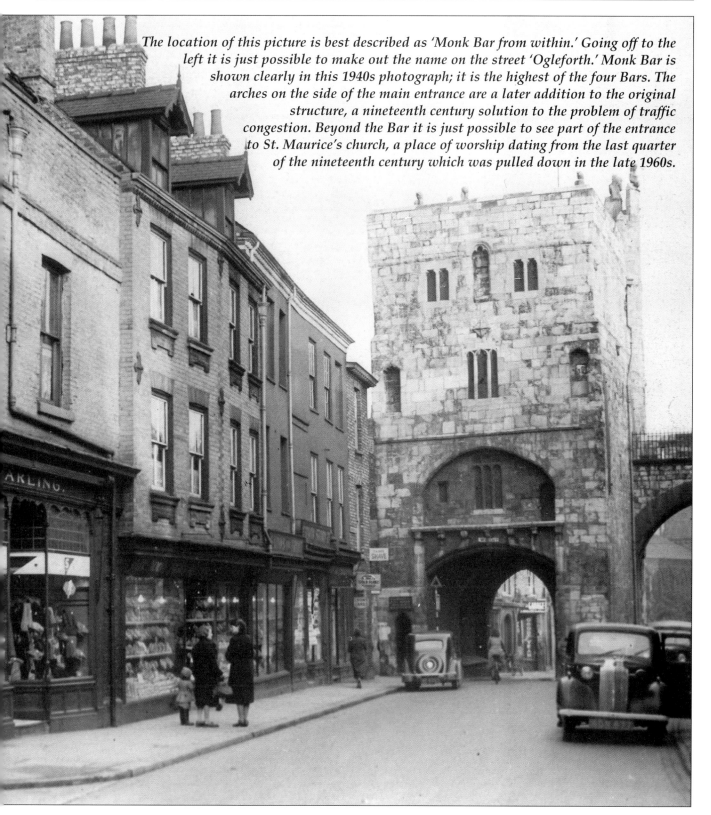

The location of this picture is best described as 'Monk Bar from within.' Going off to the left it is just possible to make out the name on the street 'Ogleforth.' Monk Bar is shown clearly in this 1940s photograph; it is the highest of the four Bars. The arches on the side of the main entrance are a later addition to the original structure, a nineteenth century solution to the problem of traffic congestion. Beyond the Bar it is just possible to see part of the entrance to St. Maurice's church, a place of worship dating from the last quarter of the nineteenth century which was pulled down in the late 1960s.

Left: Approaching Walmgate Bar from Hull Road was clearly a much more relaxed affair than is the case in modern times. This picture, featuring Lawrence Street, originates from the 1940s, and projects the atmosphere of an attractive Surrey suburb rather than the hectic arterial route which we recognise today. A variety of businesses are present here and they may serve to bring back memories for people who knew the area at the time. Austin Davison was the landlord of the Waggon and Horses (Magnet Ales) and lower down the road Harold Thornhill ran the Rose and Crown at number 13 Lawrence Street. Mr Barker ran the

tobaconnists shop and H. Chapman was the chemist at 25-28 Lawrence Street for many years.

Top left: The photographer created an artistic effect in this picture which was taken at Monk Bar. The Bar once housed prisoners in two rooms over the central arch over 400 years ago and the structure has the distinction of being the tallest of the Bars in York as well as being one of the most elegant. It is not known what the occasion was to bring this smart military band to the edge of the ominously sharp teeth of the portcullis, so if any reader can enlighten us we would be delighted to hear from you!

Wartime

Left: An unusual but very satisfying picture featuring Coney Street in the 1940s. Our eyes are drawn to The Picture House and Picture House Café on the left of the photograph. The Picture House dates from 1915 having cost £10,000 to construct. The popular place of entertainment closed in 1955 and the site was redeveloped by Woolworths. On the same side of the street was the Willow Café and The Fifty Shilling Tailors, with the Scotch Wool and Hosiery outlet further along. Three even more famous establishments can be seen on the opposite side of the street - Burtons the Tailors, H. Samuel (jewellers) and Boots the Chemists. A stroll along the street would mean passing the Yorkshire Penny Bank and the Black Swan. A couple of other points are worth a mention too; the sign bearing the large letter "S" indicated the location of the public air-raid shelter; the delivery van in the distance has clearly marked lettering on its rear showing that it belonged to F.T. Burley & Son the wholesale fruit, vegetable and flower supplier.

Above: Muriel Lyon had her ladies outfitters business on Micklegate Hill when this picture was taken sometime around 1940. A glance at the upstairs window of the shop reveals white sticky tape fixed to the windows in a cross-hatched pattern. This was done on the advice of the Ministry of Information during the Second World War and intended to limit the effects of flying glass in the event of a nearby bomb explosion.

Unmistakably Micklegate, but the paraphernalia of wartime so clearly in evidence might lead one to imagine that a film crew has staged the scene for some T.V drama. This is not the case, for the sandbags and blacked-out lamps reflect a real threat of enemy attack which was never far from the thoughts of every York resident at the time this picture was taken. The building on the right of the picture is the YWCA of course, as indicated by the large sign on the 'Barker Lane' wall of the building. The YWCA was located at No. 86 Micklegate, other business premises included Raimes and Co. the Wholesale Chemists at No. 88 -90, The Falcon Hotel at No. 94, "Maurice" (M. Newton) and the All-Night Café next door, and The Nags Head Inn at No. 100. Further still up the street could be found the Red Lion Hotel and Gordon Holmes the butcher.... among others.

"WHITE STICKY TAPE, INTENDED TO LIMIT THE EFFECTS OF FLYING GLASS, WAS FIXED TO THE WINDOWS IN A CROSS-HATCHED PATTERN"

Below: Micklegate Hill proved a challenge for the cyclists seen in this picture. The lady at the head of the group of cyclists has resorted to pushing her bike up the slope, but a young lad lower down the incline has found a more innovative solution. He is hitching a ride from the strange tractor-like vehicle crawling towards the position of the camera, holding on to the back of the machine and enjoying the ride. Behind and to the right of the pair we can see the sign belonging to Estelle the ladies hairdresser, and to the left of that is a wartime advertisement for War Bonds. The British Legion's rather grimy fascia sign is visible on the right of the photograph.

Wartime Micklegate is featured in this picture. Several clues combine here to let us know that it is indeed a wartime scene; the advertising hoarding positioned high on the building on the right, the sign with the capital 'S' on the right which indicates the location of a public air raid shelter, and the bright white anti-blast tape on many of the windows seen here.

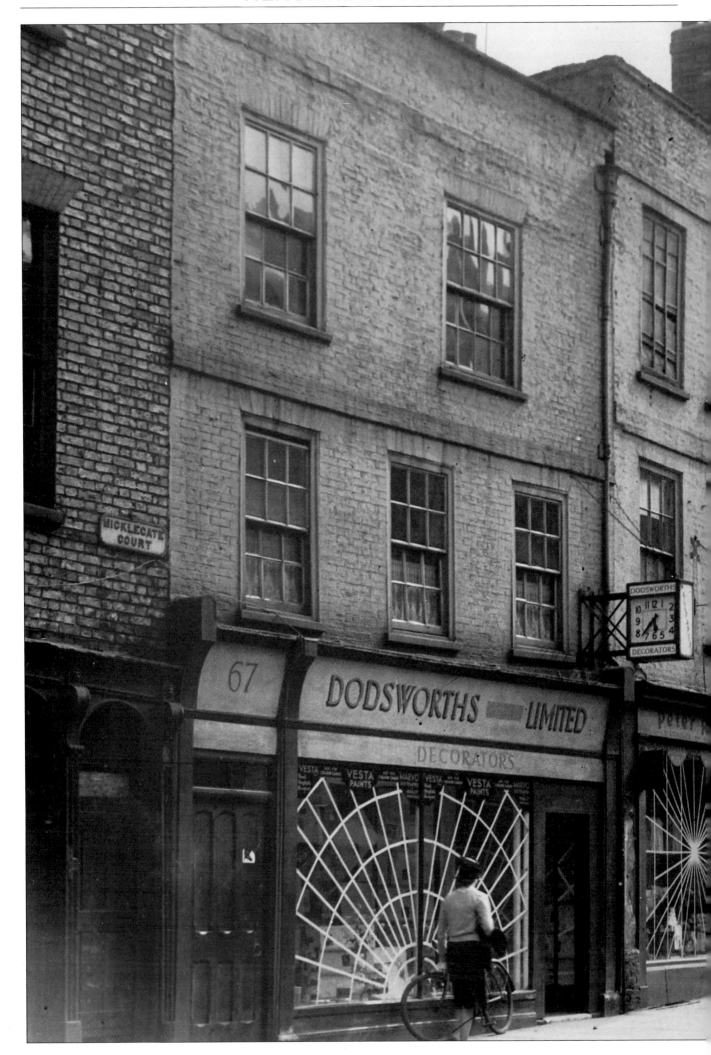

Young readers may imagine that the strange spiders-web designs on Dodsworths window and those on the adjacent retail shops had something to do with halloween. But the more mature among us recognise this as a wartime precaution against exploding bombs and the flying glass which was capable of inflicting terrible injuries hundreds of yards away from the initial impact of the bomb. Dodsworths were at number 67 Micklegate and 'Peter Rabbit' (at number 69) was the creatively-named fancy wool shop. Readers may remember Sheldon's Stores - popular Micklegate grocers trading from number 71 for many years. Less pleasant memories may be recalled by some people of the the area office of the Unemployment Benefit Board, lower down the street at 47 Micklegate.

A 1940s photograph showing Micklegate and the approach to the junction with North Street and Skeldergate. The large grey building in the picture is The Queens Hotel located at number 7 - 9 Micklegate. The unusual sign above the adjacent retail property proclaimed "We serve it differently" - this referred to the bacon shop that was popular here for many years. Leslie Soårds was the licensee of the Crown Hotel which stood next to the Cafe Royal, in front of which are a couple of boys who appear to be carrying gas masks. Further wartime clues to the date of the picture exist in the white bumper on the delightful saloon car travelling up the hill, and the group of soldiers, walking away from the camera opposite it.

Outskirts

Ask people from outside York to name ten things associated with the City and it is likely that one of them will be the area's tendency to experience serious flooding every time someone forgets to turn the bath taps off. We can only guess at the thoughts going through the minds of the people on this horse and cart as it rescues them from their water-logged homes. They were probably less than thrilled at the idea of having their moment of misery recorded for all and sundry to pore over in this press photograph. The picture dates from 1947, but it could have been taken on dozens of other occasions during the period covered by this book. The street shown here is Walker Street, a mainly residential area with only few business premises. The area was always one of the first to suffer when the Ouse rose over its banks, and it was not until the early 1990s that really effective flood control was introduced to keep the water at bay. Some readers may be able to remember the nimble fingers and barber-shop wit of Bernard Hill, as he created dozens of *short back-and-sides* each week at his shop at number 16.

New houses being built in the Acomb area are featured here. The scenes date from the early 1930s. Notice how the builder had introduced an element of variety into the design of these homes - some with gables, others with porches or arches, and everyone of them the object of the hopes and aspirations of many local couples, eager to find their dream home. The pattern of housing distribution has changed over the years in York, though arguably not to the same extent as in more obviously industrial towns. As public transport has developed (and later, the ownership of personal means of transport) it has been possible for people to live further away from their place of employment, hence the growth of 'suburbs' such as the houses shown here. Simpson Brothers were the reputable York builders responsible for creating these desirable homes. They worked from premises at Vine Street in Bishopthorpe Road and Manor Drive at Acomb. These pictures date from May 1931, a time when Oswald Mosley was just founding the New Party, along the lines of the Fascist Movement, while a coalition government was being formed by Ramsay MacDonald. It was the year that the Empire State Building was completed in New York, and, also in America, the gangster 'Al' Capone was jailed for income tax evasion.

Bottom: The bottom of Holgate Hill took on a wide river-like appearance when the rain came down in the flooding of 1947. Pity the poor residents with their soaked carpets and furniture which would take weeks to dry out properly - if it was not completely ruined in the first place. And the damp smell, often reminiscent of a large wet dog, would take even longer to get rid of. House contents insurance would not provide the safeguard that it does today for many of the people who suffered - most couldn't afford it in any case. At least the children seem to be having some fun in the water, but the ex-army truck in the distance looks well and truly bogged down.

Right: Feeding the ducks in Rowntree Park has been a popular pass-time for York's youngsters ever since the park opened in 1921. The park was formally opened by Mr. Joseph Rowntree, the Chairman of the famous confectionery firm, in July of that year when the title deeds to the facility were handed over to Alderman Edward Walker, the Mayor of York. This photograph was taken around 70 years ago, in 1931. The park was donated in memory of the Rowntrees staff who had given their lives or been injured in the First World War. The park covered an area of 17 acres at Clementhorpe and included a 'wading' pool, a 'sandbeach', two bowling greens, hockey and football pitches and a cafe. The park has been a jewel in the crown of York's leisure facilities ever since.

Around the city streets

The old and the new contrast sharply in this 1955 view of York. The building on the right is Cussins the electrical retailers of Kings Square, and a delightful Armstrong Siddley saloon car can be seen passing in front of it. Just across the road is the busy corner site of the Kettering Boot Company. Further along the road, opposite the Petergate Fish Restaurant is the much-loved Merrimans' store. It was always something of a challenge as a pedestrian making your way through this area before the planners outlawed the motorcar.

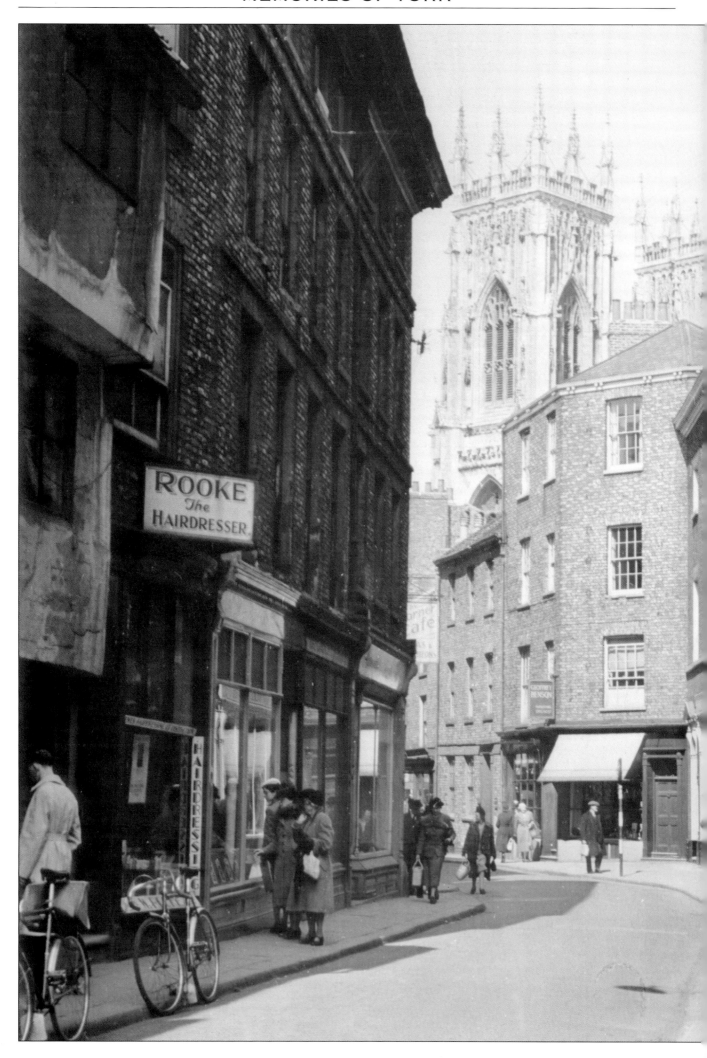

Left: An almost artistic view along Petergate captured on a warm sunny day, with the Minster peeping over the rooftops in the background. Geoffrey Benson the furniture specialists can be seen in the distance, as can the Corner Café. Rooke's 'hairdressers of distinction' is on the left of the picture, near the parked bicycles. In a city bursting with history Petergate can rightly claim to be one of the most historically significant parts of York. High Petergate contains the birthplace of the traitor Guy Fawkes - Young's Hotel - and the area was the very centre of military activity in Roman times.

Above: The angle of the camera used to take this picture gives the buildings along Stonegate an imposing, or even overbearing appearance. This is probably a 1940s image, and local directories from the time suggest that this part of York was a centre for many small businesses involved in service industries of one kind or another. Evidence of this can be seen in this photograph. The large sign on the right of the picture shows the location of Caroline Hall the Chiropodist. To the right of that is Kleneright the Drycleaners, proudly boasting the use of Ozolene to clean suits and plain dresses at prices starting from 3/6. The H.M.V shop can be seen on the left of the picture - note the delightful 'His Masters Voice' advertising sign on the side of it. Many other service-oriented companies operated from this area, including printers, estate agents, insurance firms, a solicitor, dressmakers, auctioneers and a doctor. Right in the distance the distinctive overhead marking the location of Ye Olde Starre Inn, York's oldest public house, can be seen. Stonegate is well known as the location of the house of the parents of Guy Fawkes.

This very nostalgic photograph features Pavement and dates from the 1950s. The Army and Navy Stores can be seen on the corner of Pavement and Fossgate and the picture is given an almost three dimensional effect by the presence of the motorcars and pedestrians at various distances from the camera. A reminder of York's ancient history is present in the form of the grey outline of All Saints Church, in the distance. The church is distinctive with its lantern tower, designed to guide worshippers into the city at night in olden times. It is said that All Saints is built on the former site of an ancient church dating from the seventh century.

The sharply-gabled roof-tops on the commercial properties here make a vivid contrast with the Minster in the background in this picture from the 1950s. A variety of small businesses are featured, including Rookes the hairdresser and E.M Newsham the Grocers and Provisioners. Approaching the camera a cyclist, complete with trailer attached to his bike, is making steady progress along the route.

Below: A thoughtfully composed photograph designed to contrast the 'old' and the 'new' as it appeared to passers-by in the 1940s. The towers of The Minster have a very graceful and dignified air about them as they look out across these more functional commercial properties of Petergate. The scene is given a nostalgic 'feel' to it by the 1930s motor car in the distance and the large wheeled cart beyond it which would have been the sole means of transport for many of York's traders at the time. V. Dawson had a popular hairdressing business along the left of the street for many years, opposite the Little Brass Shop which proudly advertised its antique and modern furniture.

Below: There are few 'modern' buildings in the City of York which are as graceful and quietly dignified as this one at St. Leonard's. This late 1940s photograph demonstrates just how little the property has changed from that time to this, though the volume of traffic passing the building is one obvious exception. On the wall of the building, on the left of the picture is the sign indicating the location of Museum Street. On the right of the picture, opposite the St. Leonard's building, one can just make out the sign on the side of the Theatre Royal. Of course, in modern times St. Leonard's is the 'home' of many Council departments and offices, but at the time this picture was taken there were many more varied organisations located here, including Smithson, Teasdale and Hewitt's Solicitors, Robert Hill the dentist, Dr. Gerald Hughes, F. Kilner the optician and H.Q of the Yorkshire Agricultural Society.

Above: The Golden Fleece at number 16 Pavement is featured in this picture, along with Currys cycle and radio shop to the right of it at number 12. Many readers might be surprised at the seemingly humble origins of this now popular and highly successful electrical retailer. It was, however, not unusual for cycle shops to branch out into the field of radio sales in the 1920s and 1930s. Sir Thomas Herbert's house is shown in restored condition and a selection of 1960s motor vehicles add to the nostalgic appeal of the picture.

"THE ORIGINS OF THE SHAMBLES CAN BE TRACED BACK AT LEAST A THOUSAND YEARS"

Below: This excellent photograph gives a clear impression of what life was like along The Shambles before the age of tourism transformed it. The origin of The Shambles can be traced back at least a thousand years, and we know that it was rebuilt substantially in the 1400s. This picture dates from the 1940s and depicts a grimy, if not grim scene with a handful of children showing the signs of the poverty they were exposed to. The name *Shambles* relates to areas' traditional butchers' trade. At the time this picture was taken there were 41 addresses listed in a local trade directory from the time. Of these 20 were businesses, and 10 of them were butchers shops. Each of the following retail trades was represented by one property along The Shambles: An antique dealer, a radio shop, a confectioner, a brass fitter, a greengrocer, a dressmaker, a jeweller, a boot repairer, a hairdresser and a tailor. In addition we noticed the discreet sign designed to attract 'victims' to the rooms occupied by 'Madame Young Royal Palmist.' On the right of the picture the oval advertising sign promotes the use of Siemens Pearl and Opal lamps - or *lightbulbs* in modern parlance. There is a hint of irony here as we look along the ancient trading corridor, for *Siemens*, a German company, is the oldest trading organisation in the world.

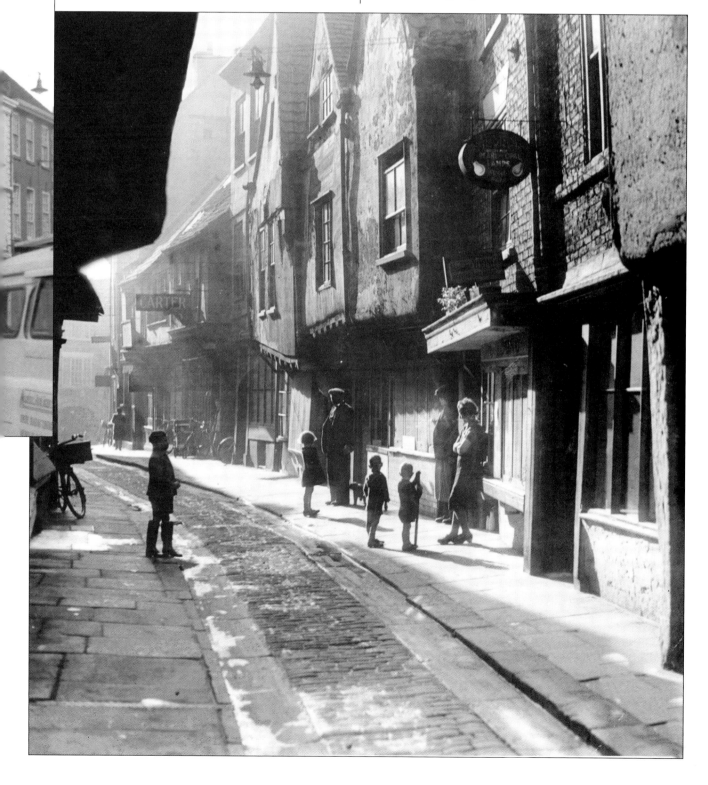

Above: The market area is often the focal point of activity and commercial life in a typical town or city. Of course, York has other places within the city walls which could claim to be the centre of activity, but in the heyday of the Parliament Street Market the area was 'up there' with the best of them. This delightful scene dates from September 1961 (it is always so much more satisfying to know the month and year when an old photograph was taken!) and many nostalgic elements are present; the old underground toilets with their thick glass roof windows designed to let light through from the pavement, the rows of (mainly British) motorcylces and scooters and the sea of canvas-topped market stalls which literally run right up to the horizon. Lots of well-known department stores and other household names from the retail world can be discerned too in the scene from around 40 years ago. Of course, market trading had been going on from this location for many years. The first market took place here in 1836, just three years after Parliament Street itself was created.

Above right: 1940s Micklegate and a scene which will be familiar to most people. The character of the street remains to the time of writing, though the businesses have changed hands many time since the photograph was taken. Hobsons fish and chip shop can be seen on the extreme right of the picture. Birdsall the watchmaker had a small shop at number 91, with F. Greaves the painter next door. Readers may recall the shop along here with the strange (for the time) name of *Peter Rabbit*. The shop was listed as a 'fancy wool shop' in a directory from the time, and was not, as you could be forgiven for thinking, concerned with selling Beatrix Potter merchandise. The large light-coloured sign just right of centre indicates the location of James Coombes the boot repairer. His business claimed to be the "pioneers of the quick repair service."

The White Horse at number 22 Coppergate is shown at the bottom right hand corner of this picture. Several other public houses could be found in the area, including The Yorkshireman Inn (at number 10), the Three Tuns at number 14, and the Market Tavern at number 26 Coppergate. Here were based several local departments of the government, including the Ministry of Education, the Ministry of Supply and the Ministry of Pensions and Social Security. Further along the street, at number 24, were the offices of the Provincial Insurance Company Ltd. On the corner of the street it may just be possible to see the sports outfitters known as T. J. Hooke and Son.

Above: Darling, Wood and Anfield were Jewellers located at number 20 Coney Street, the shop next door to the timber-framed building on the corner. Countless devoted couples have gazed excitedly into this jewellers' shop window, studying the sparkling engagement and wedding rings, so carefully laid out there, in eager anticipation of the life they would spend together. A story repeated at every jewellers in every town throughout the country, and noticed by anonymous passers-by who once shared the same dreams. This picture dates from August 1964 and also features Thomas Cooks the travel agents who would have been happy to supply the honeymoon, and Bennett's camera shop, the starting point for everyone who wanted to take the best wedding photos!

Right: Gillygate, with dustbins awaiting collection on a fairly quiet day. Thank goodness too, for the bins would have been nasty little obstacles for anyone with less than tip-top vision. Notice the fruit and vegetable shop on the right of the picture at number 10. It operated under the name of D.R. Sadd for many years, in the era of 'proper shopping' -

long before the days of out of town supermarkets. There is a wartime 'feel' to the photograph created by the anti-bomb-blast tape on some of the windows and the shrouded car headlights on the only vehicle in the picture. How many readers remember the Viola Café which incorporated a bakers shop at number 12? ... or Frank Harris the ladies and childrens' outfitters at number 14? It must have been difficult for these little businesses to make a living during the war years.

Top right: This charming photograph dates from 1955 and shows the approach to the Minster from Museum Street, with the Prudential Assurance building on the right of the scene. There is only a handful of people in the picture, and the people shown are obviously unaware that their presence is being recorded for us to see over 40 years later.

An elevated view across the city in this photograph taken from the top of York Minster. The huge cooling tower on the left of the picture looks extremely out of place in the historic city. This may be the case with this and other structures which are necessary to bring us our services and power supplies, and it has always been necessary to find a balance between the visually pleasing and practically essential. Over the years the population has tended to move out of the once poorly-appointed housing stock within the city walls to the modern housing estates located in the suburbs on the outskirts of the city.

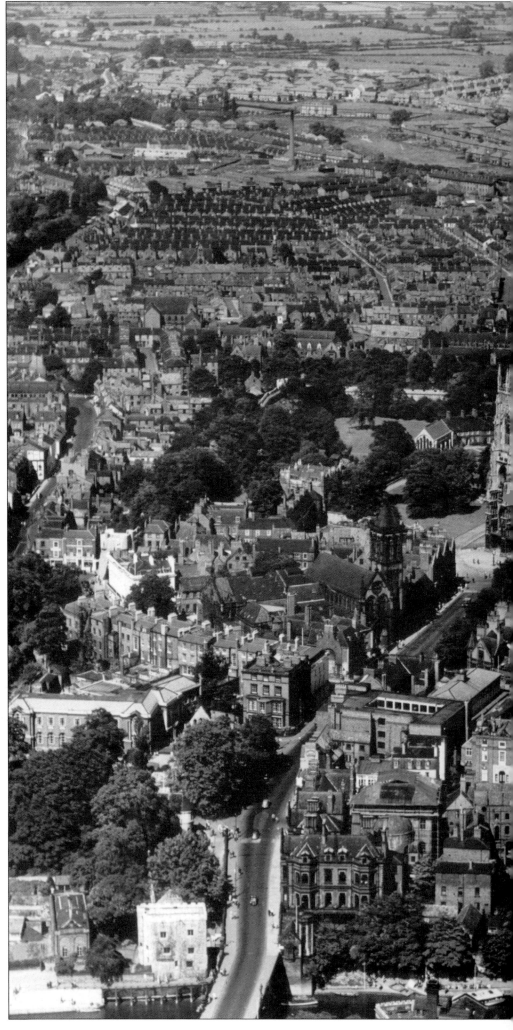

The centrepiece of this view is, not surprisingly, The Minster. The photograph demonstrates the sheer bulk of York's most precious monument and the way it dominates the architecture of the city. The picture was taken from an altitude of 1600 ft from an aircraft in 1951. The Lendal Bridge can just be seen at the bottom of the picture, on the left, with Museum Street going up towards the Minster. The picture gives a good view of the properties around Stonegate, Petergate, Coney Street, and the Museum area, as well as the residential housing on the outskirts of the city to the east.

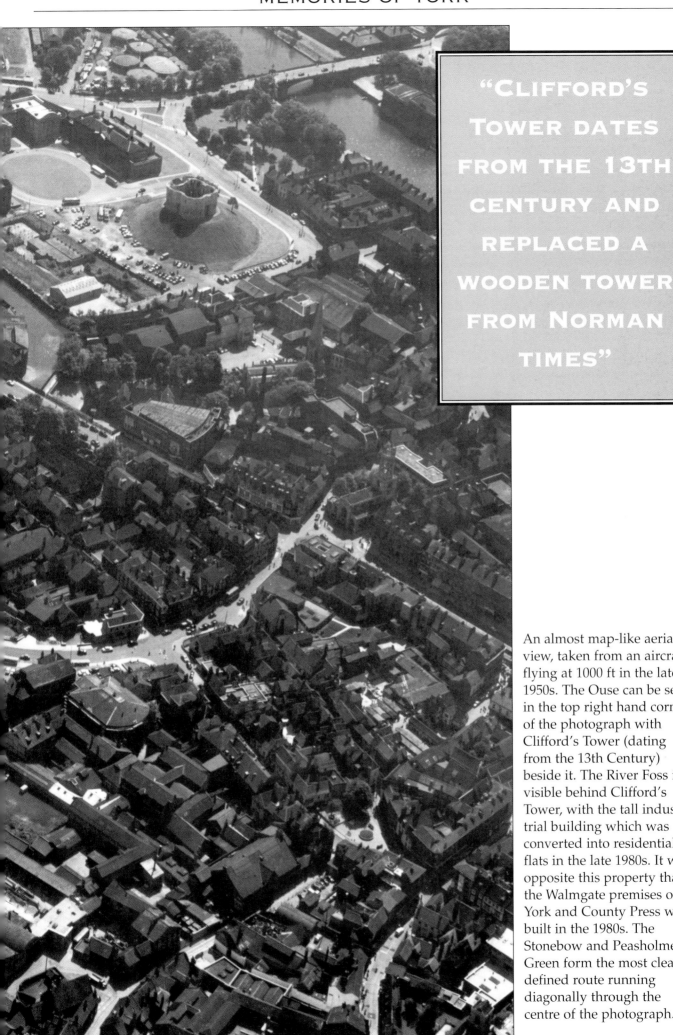

"CLIFFORD'S TOWER DATES FROM THE 13TH CENTURY AND REPLACED A WOODEN TOWER FROM NORMAN TIMES"

An almost map-like aerial view, taken from an aircraft flying at 1000 ft in the late 1950s. The Ouse can be seen in the top right hand corner of the photograph with Clifford's Tower (dating from the 13th Century) beside it. The River Foss is visible behind Clifford's Tower, with the tall industrial building which was converted into residential flats in the late 1980s. It was opposite this property that the Walmgate premises of York and County Press were built in the 1980s. The Stonebow and Peasholme Green form the most clearly defined route running diagonally through the centre of the photograph.

A delightful view of the centre of York which dates from May 1959. Many changes have taken place to the city in the 40 years or so since that time. The gentle curve of the River Ouse dominates the lower half of the picture and two of York's bridges, the Lendal (on the left) and the Ouse (on the right) are clearly in view. Rougier Street and North Street can be seen on the right of the photograph along with the historic buildings just a short distance across the water between Coney Street and the Ouse. As a point of reference, the roof of the Minster can be seen half way up the picture on the left. The bottom left hand corner of the photograph shows the Museum Gardens - the grounds where once stood St, Mary's Benedictine Abbey. This is, of course, the location of the world-famous York Mystery Plays.

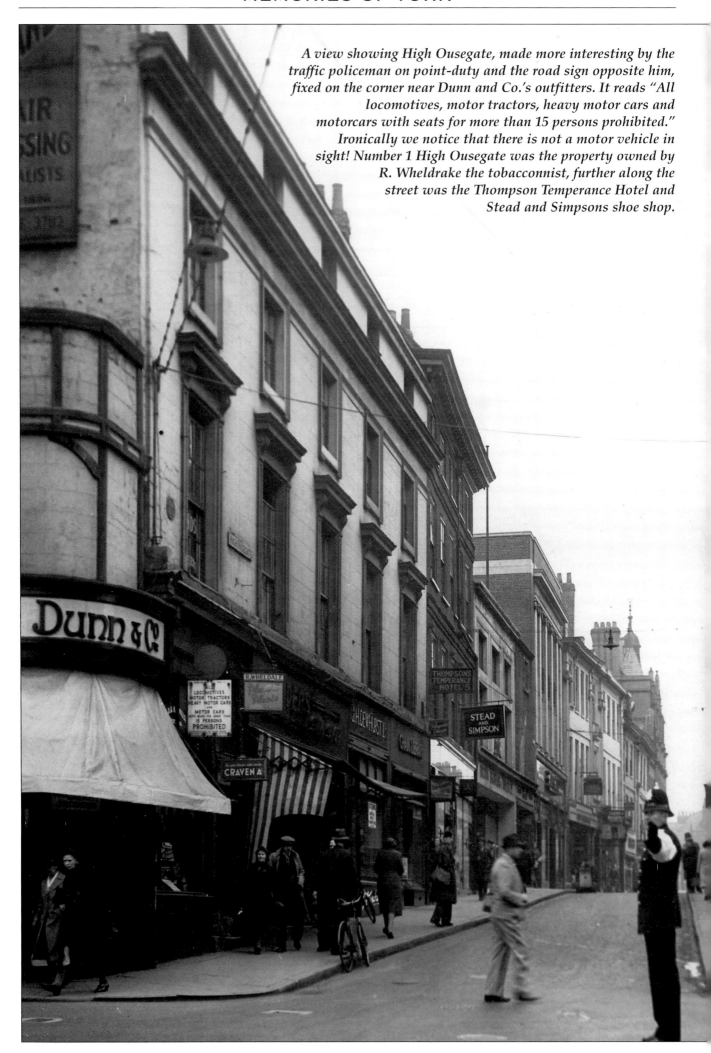

A view showing High Ousegate, made more interesting by the traffic policeman on point-duty and the road sign opposite him, fixed on the corner near Dunn and Co.'s outfitters. It reads "All locomotives, motor tractors, heavy motor cars and motorcars with seats for more than 15 persons prohibited." Ironically we notice that there is not a motor vehicle in sight! Number 1 High Ousegate was the property owned by R. Wheldrake the tobacconnist, further along the street was the Thompson Temperance Hotel and Stead and Simpsons shoe shop.

Below: The corner of Rougier Street and Wellington Row is featured in this picture from the 1950s. Note the R.A.C. sign on the railings on the right of the picture indicating the location of the 'Car Sleeper Loading Dock' at the railway station. The once-busy corner site in the picture was occupied by T.H Lumb the newsagent for many years from where he would conduct a thriving trade in morning and evening newspapers bought by eager railway commutors. This picture affords a good view of the Pickfords depot and Central Garage further along the street.

Bottom: A panorama across the rooftops in 1950s York is afforded by this archers-eye view. The picture brings back memories of the York we knew around half a century ago, and the cute, post war motorcars in the foreground add to those nostalgic feelings. The garage beneath the battlements was an Austin dealership. Very few images of York are complete without the presence of the Minster, and this picture is no exception.

Main picture: A delightful picture featuring Collingbournes' Acomb motor dealership at 37 The Green. We should take care not to be fooled by the obvious age of these four lovely old motors. Closer inspection reveals that the veteran cars are taking part in some kind of motoring event, each carrying a number relating to their entry in the run, with proud owners standing beside them ready for the off. It is likely that picture dates from the 1950s. By this time Collingbournes' were involved in T.V and electrical supplies, as well as being Ford and Fordson (tractor) dealers from their Greenside Garage.

Inset: Certain to be of interest to those keen on motor transport, this picture shows the owner and staff of E. Collinbournes' garage in Acomb. the picture probably dates from the 1920s.

On the move

A local directory from the time lists the main business activities conducted by Collinbournes' as being motor engineers, motorcar dealers, motor accessories, cycle and radio suppliers. It is known that the firm went on to sell and repair televisions in later years. It is interesting to notice that the business clearly incorporated an outlet for groceries and sweets in this picture - long before the marketing people equipped every branded petrol filling station with everything needed to rival grocers and corner shops. These petrol pumps look interesting too. The bulbous illuminated signs on top of them are at least eight feet off the ground - and each pump is complete with a swinging arm used to get the flexible rubber part of the device to whichever side of the vehicle contained the filler cap.

Above: The development of different forms of public transport is closely linked with feelings of nostalgia, even among people far too young to remember travelling on them. Most of us remember conversations with parents or grandparents about *their* journeys on the trams. This picture suggests that the excitement and romance associated with tram travelling would have been offset by the passengers' exposure to the elements. Still, the experience would have been better than the alternative - walking - and the service was well-used. This number 17 tram operated by City of York Tramways was crewed by two young ladies and carried advertisements for Brookes the Chemist at 57 Blossom Street and a play showing at the Theatre Royal called 'Brave Women Who Wait.' In the 1920s the trams operated services each weekday from 8.00 am until 11.00 pm at 7 1/2 minute intervals. One or two special trams operated a service intended to get 'early' workers to their places of employment before 8.00am. On Sundays the service began at 2.00pm and ran until 10.00pm.

Below: A number 24 tram on the South Bank route is nicely framed in this picture fom the 1920s. Note the telegraph wires high above the level of the electric overhead cables. York's first electric trams were introduced on a service between the city centre and Fulford in 1910. The electric tram era in York lasted just a quarter of a century, rather less than was the case in other northern towns and cities. The last electric tram ran in November 1935 and was driven on its last journey, by one Mr. Stewart, the man who drove the Civic Party on the city's first electric tram. The introduction of electric trams an the laying of miles of track through the city caused great upheaval for a year between 1909 and 1910. It really was a major civil engineering project, completed with few of the mechanical aids that modern contractors take advantage of today, in an operation mirrored in hundreds of communities throughout Britain at this time.

> "THE ELECTRIC TRAM ERA IN YORK LASTED JUST A QUARTER OF A CENTURY, THE LAST ONE RUNNING IN NOVEMBER 1935"

Left: A snowy scene with an uncertain date of origin, but the subject matter is unmistakably the side of the railway station with a handful of motor buses battling against the elements. Some of the advertising signs make interesting reading for the modern transport user; 'Leeds 2/3 .... in 30 minutes' - 'by L.N.E.R Express Train - the quickest way.' ...And 'Unite the family - send a railway ticket as a greeting card 1p per mile... Any Train to Anywhere.' For those on a small budget a return evening excursion to Leeds could be made for 1s 3d - less than 7p in modern money!

Below left: A pleasant view of the interior of York Railway Station which dates from the late 1950s. The present railway station dates from 1877, having replaced an earlier structure which resembled nothing more than a draughty engine shed, staffed by a booking clerk and the company secretary. This was the starting place for the first rail journey from York, in 1839. It was a bumpy return journey to Copmanthorpe which took 40 minutes and heralded the beginning of York's railway age.

Railway buffs from far and wide are drawn to the City by the marvellous National Railway Museum located on Leeman Road, and it is fitting that those of them who arrive by rail are met by such a magnificent structure as the present railway station.

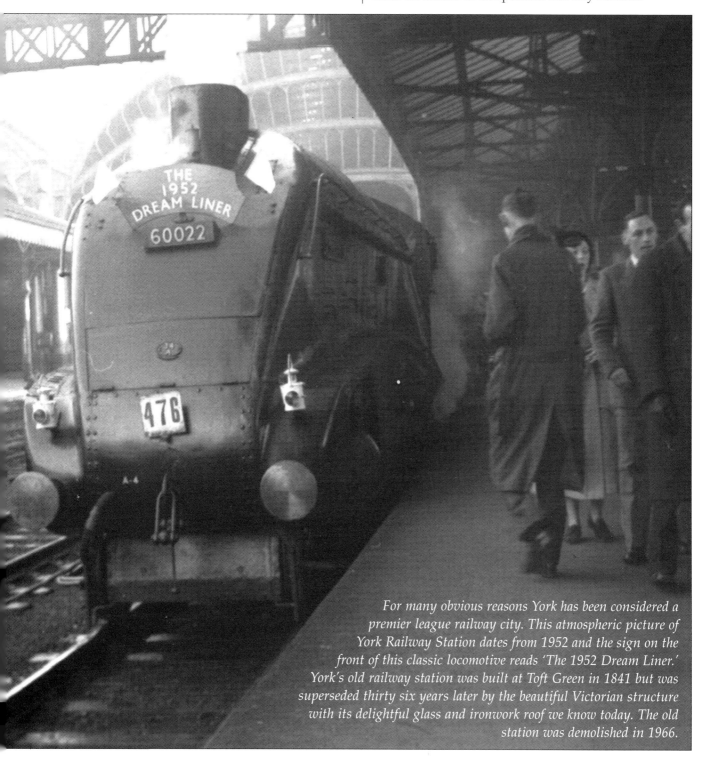

For many obvious reasons York has been considered a premier league railway city. This atmospheric picture of York Railway Station dates from 1952 and the sign on the front of this classic locomotive reads 'The 1952 Dream Liner.' York's old railway station was built at Toft Green in 1841 but was superseded thirty six years later by the beautiful Victorian structure with its delightful glass and ironwork roof we know today. The old station was demolished in 1966.

Below: To those of us who were less familiar with the intricate goings-on in the railway industry there always seemed to be lots of 'waiting around' by the staff in a typical large railway station. This picture captures a scene from the 1950s when this phenomenon was particularly apparent. The figures in the picture are mainly B.R staff, with only a couple of passengers present. The trolleys on the platform appear to be carrying sacks of mail. In the era featured here, in the days before Britain had an extensive motorway network, the railway played an even more important role in the distribution of many staple products - including many foodstuffs and newspapers for example. The improvement in the country's road network and the closure, in the 1960s, of many smaller stations under *Beeching* resulted in a setback in the importance of rail transport for many of these goods.

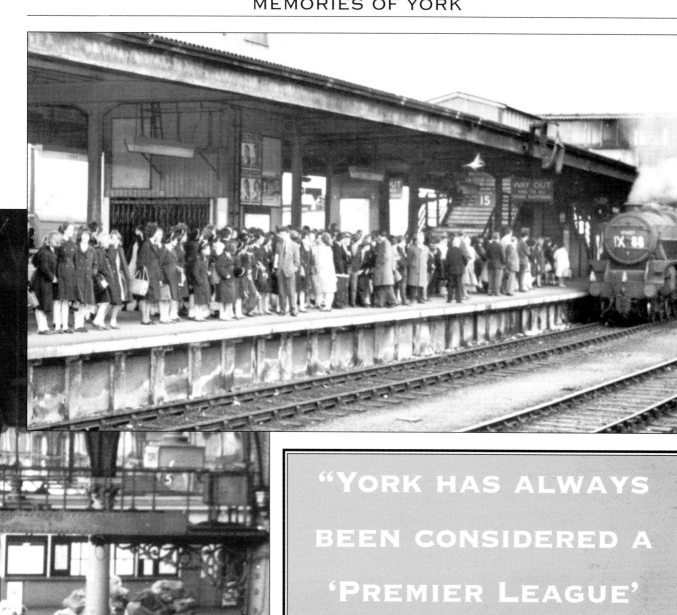

"YORK HAS ALWAYS BEEN CONSIDERED A 'PREMIER LEAGUE' RAILWAY CITY"

Above: A school teacher looks on anxiously as his pupils stand beside the platform on York Railway Station. There must have been around 100 excited children waiting for their train - all equipped with duffle bags (they wouldn't be seen dead with one now!) and packed lunches for their day out. It is not clear to us which school these children attended, and of course it is possible that they belonged to a school outside York and were visiting the city because of its historic nature. The photograph is given added appeal to those interested in nostalgia by the presence of the steam engine. There are few things quite as inspiring as sounds and smell generated by these powerful locomotives, and few things quite so capable of reminding us of happy times from the past.

Above: Everyone in this 1950s picture was going about their business, seemingly unaware of the photographer recording the scene for us to see around 50 years later. Note the two men with their cycles in the foreground; one is holding the others' bike to enable him to mount it, complete with a bread tray on his head!

Half a dozen or so vehicles add to the atmosphere in the photograph, especially the small Austin saloon about to turn right at the junction, and the ubiquitous Morris half ton van to the left of it, a favourite of the Post Office for many years and familiar sight in scores of period black and white films.

"YORK'S NARROW STREETS HAVE ALWAYS CAUSED PROBLEMS FOR MOTORISTS"

Below: York's narrow streets have always been something of a bottleneck - not that they are trouble free for motorists in modern times. But even in the days before the City was swamped with tourists in the summer and every Bank Holiday there were problems for local people travelling to and from work - and for business people making and receiving deliveries. This picture dates from the 1950s - the truck on the right of the picture belonged to Hammond's United Breweries and would no doubt have been making deliveries to a local cellar. The Ford Popular was of the 'sit up and beg' variety which provided affordable transportation for the masses in the 1950s.

A variety of motor transport combine to thoroughly clog up the route through St. Saviourgate in this 1950s photograph. To modern eyes perhaps the most interesting mode of transport in the picture is the machine ridden by the gentleman in the light-coloured raincoat on the left.

It looks like a bicycle, but closer inspection reveals a tiny cowl on top of the front wheel. This contained a minuscule petrol engine which would drive the cycle along via a rubber wheel which pressed on the cycle tyre. A variety of 'cycle wheels' and 'cycle motors' could be bought around this time to convert cycles to mopeds. Note the semaphore indicator on the Morris saloon in the centre of the picture.

A view along Pavement, York's first paved street, with the graceful lines of All Saint's Church rising high above street level in this distance. In geographical terms this is the very centre of the walled city and it is appropriate therefore that many historic streets and monuments are located here. Whip-Ma-Whop-Ma-Gate, the city's shortest street which derives its name from the time, in the sixteenth century, when villains would be whipped along the street as a punishment. Of course The Shambles, York's most historic retail area dating back in its present form to the fourteenth century, also begins at Pavement. Bringing us right up to date, the commercial vehicles in the scene, especially this coachbuilt box van are certain to evoke feelings of nostalgia.

At leisure

Below: A pleasant rowing trip was the order of the day for this lucky pair when this picture was taken in the early 1960s. York has always had so much to offer in terms of leisure and recreation and long-time residents are often a little guilty of taking it for granted. This photograph contains nothing in the way of grand monuments or well-known buildings, but it still manages to convey a delightful feeling of calm and relaxation which is characteristic of many areas in the city.

Above: River navigation has long been an attractive aspect of York and this 1950s photograph epitomises the pleasure that the Ouse has brought to countless thousands of people over the years. The Ouse follows a curvaceous course to the Humber and the North Sea and is spanned by no less than five bridges on its route through the city. The Ouse Bridge was built in 1810, making it the oldest of the remaining crossing points. The Lendal and Skeldergate Bridges date from the second half of the last century. 1816 saw the first steamboat on the Ouse, to the delight of thousands of sightseers who turned out to see it. The vessel, Waterloo was a familiar sight on the river for many years. Pleasure boat trips to Bishopthorpe have been popular for many decades.

> ## "THE OUSE FOLLOWS A CURVACEOUS COURSE TO THE HUMBER AND THE NORTH SEA"

Above: A tranquil scene dating from the 1950s which features King's Square and a small group of railway workers enjoying the summer sunshine. The square was made possible, if that is the term, by the demolition of the Holy Trinity Church and takes its name from Viking times as it once regarded as the home of Viking Kings. York's *Viking* period lasted for less than 100 years and spanned the time between about A.D 867 and A.D 954, not that this fact would have been uppermost in the minds of the people seen here, taking advantage of a relatively quiet oasis in the hustle and bustle of one of the busiest areas in the city. For many years the tranquillity afforded by the clearing which is King's Square has been offset by its use by street entertainers, eager to earn a pound or two with their short, open-air shows for passing tourists.

"THE TRANQUILITY OFFERED BY KINGS SQUARE HAS SOMETIMES BEEN OFFSET BY STREET ENTERTAINERS WITH THEIR OPEN-AIR SHOWS."

Below: Hunter and Smallpage Ltd had an up-market furniture shop in Goodramgate, York. This advertisement from the mid-1950s shows a display of furniture available in their shop, being 'modelled' in a setting which featured playwright Michael Pertwee and his actress wife Valerie French. Note the small television receiver to the left of the couple. It looks almost comic now, but a set of these (small) dimensions would have been very advanced - and desirable at the time.

Above: This picture is less than 30 years old and would not feature in many 'nostalgia' books on account of its 'youth' and the absence of penny-farthings, bowler hats and trams. Yet the Odeon and the other picture houses which competed with it in York are as much a part of most people's memories as wartime rationing, the York Herald, the old railway station and, dare we say it, the Minster itself.

At the time of writing the Odeon still stands on Blossom Street and, superficially at least, looks strikingly similar to this picture from 1974. When this picture was taken two James Bond movies were being shown there, 'You Only Live Twice' and 'Thunderball.' There have been many picture houses in York and the York area over the last century. Their popularity rose and fell over time, but when most homes acquired a television set the days of most of them were numbered. 'Bingo' saved many buildings, and carpet and other retailers saved many more, but the Odeon endured the lean times and, like many other cinemas is now enjoying the revival in the popularity of this type of entertainment.

We can think of at least eight other cinemas which have provided entertainment in the York area, including: The Electric (Fossgate); The Rialto (Fishergate); the Picture House (Coney street); St. George's Hall Cinema (Castlegate); The Tower Super Cinema (New Street); the Regent Cinema (Acomb); The Regal (Piccadilly) and The Clifton Cinema at Clifton. Fond memories of courting days and first dates are prompted by these names, not to mention the Saturday morning matinees when harassed usherettes and over stretched managers would struggle to keep order before the lights went down. We remember it well.

Right: Steeped in history, this delightful picture was taken on Blossom Street in the 1920s. The photograph is interesting in its own right, but is made more so when one realises that this is the site now occupied by the Odeon cinema. The Crescent Café and Danse Salon offered a wide range of attractions and services, and was not shy about shouting about them in the adverting material which 'dressed' the

building. Among the tempting facilities were rooms for dances, luncheons and teas, light refreshments, whist drives, social meetings, and birthday parties. There are advertisements for departures by road to London and it seems likely that this would have been a staging point for these long journeys. Note the public weighing scale on the right, where those with a halfpenny and a brass neck could weigh themselves beside the normally busy road. Rowntrees clear gums are advertised on the high-level hoarding as is Oxo with the slogan 'and so to bed.'

Shopping spree

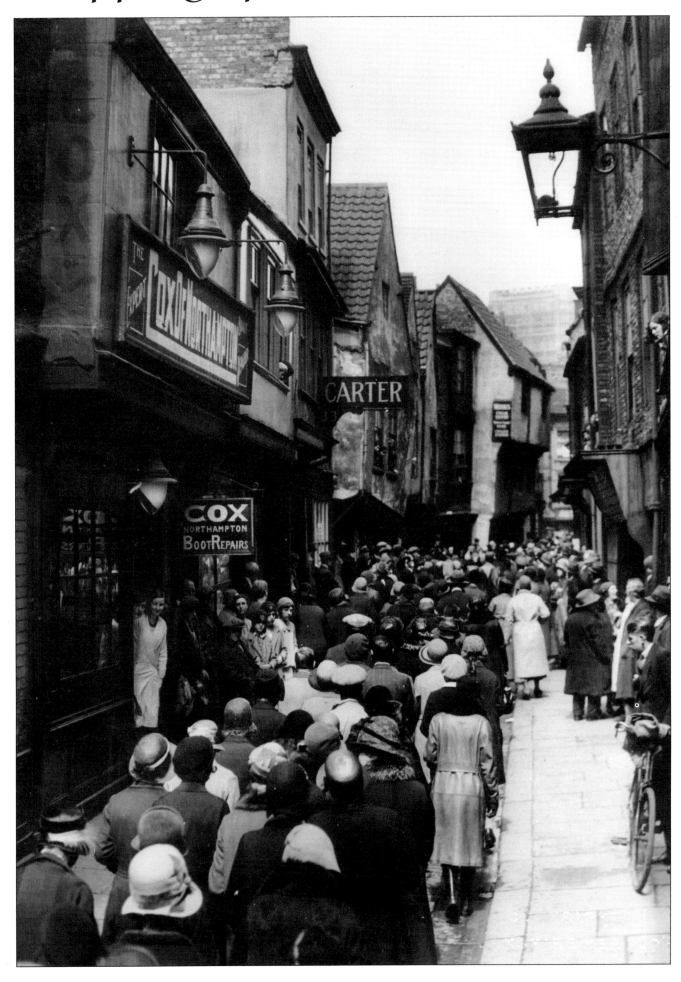

Far left: This very atmospheric picture shows a procession making its way along the narrow thoroughfare we know as The Shambles. It is thought to date from the 1930s or early 1940s and the walkers are heading in the direction of King's Square. The main business in view is the 'expert boot repairing' shop run by William Frederick Cox of Northampton. Note too the half-whited out lamps designed to illuminate his sign without dazzling the residents in the properties on the other side of the narrow passageway. Further along The Shambles is Carters the butchers, based at number 33. The final piece of street furniture worthy of note is the marvellous gas lamp high above the

passers-by on the right of the picture. It would have been considered to be commonplace and ugly by most people when this scene was captured - but now it would be thought of as a highly prized curiosity in the garden of many grand houses. How times have changed!

Below left: Long before the days of the modern super-market, and the tendency of most people to do their *weekly* shopping by car, it was normal for large grocers and 'provisions merchants' like this Henry Coning store to be distributed around towns and cities to enable housewives and housekeepers to have access to their weekly supplies. Of course, most, if not all grocers, butchers and fishmongers had at least one delivery boy equipped with a bike with a large whicker basket attached to make home deliveries. As we write, many large food retailers are introducing home deliveries for their customers, *they have seen the past - and it works.*

Below: "Sleep back your energy tonight" proclaims the Ovaltine poster on the side of John Cross' grocery shop. This busy view along Petergate has the towers of York Minster in the background, looking down the busy Petergate. Many familiar landmarks can be seen, familiar that is, to people who remember shopping in this area in the late 1950s. As a point of reference, the street leading off to the left (beneath the Ovaltine sign) is Church Street, and on the opposite side of the road is Goodramgate of course. In the distance the Fox Inn can be seen, as can the Petergate Fish Restaurant one of the many busy eating places patronised by tourists and local people alike, especially at lunch times. By the time this picture was taken the street had already been designated as 'one way' - a wise precaution in view of the narrowness of the thoroughfare.

Below: This view along Petergate was recorded in the mid 1960s. The date is relatively easy to determine from the delightful motorcars (an Austin A40 and a Vauxhall Victor saloon), both apparently in 'mint' condition. Several small traders' businesses are clearly in view, but the one guaranteed to bring back the fondest memories is the business operated by Ernest Precious in the toy and model shop previously located in Swinegate. The 1940s saw relocation to Petergate and a reign over the hearts and aspirations of every York youngster for a period of almost 50 years. The shop closed in the late 1980s. Further along the street Scott's the pork butchers could be found, and further still J.C. & M. Wroe's provisions and grocery store was popular with York's housewives.

Right: There have been many changes to the appearance of Coney Street since this photograph was taken. The picture shows New Street on the left indicated by the sign firmly fixed to what was then Martins Bank. Another sign on the front of the bank boldly advertises War Bonds, giving the appearance of the bank something approaching the branch managed by Captain Mainwaring in *Dad's Army.* Next door to the bank at number 13 Coney Street was *Strouds* - the 'Registry Office for Servants.' The blacked-out lamp on the motorcar outside Singers the Dyers suggests that this picture was taken sometime during the 1939-45 conflict. In the far distance the vertical sign

denoting the location of the Picture House and Picture House Café can just be seen. There were, as now, many well-known retail names along Coney Street at the time this picture was taken, including Stead and Simpson, W.H. Smiths the stationers and bookshop, The Fifty Shilling Tailors and the Yorkshire Herald. Of course, the area has been transformed in recent times with the pedestrianisation of the busy street.

August 1964 and a mature gentleman studies the display in the window of the House of Bewlay. The picture was taken along Coney Street of course, and many familiar shops an be seen in the photograph. Among these is Thomas Cooks travel agents, Darling, Wood and Anfield (the jewellers) and Leaders Fashions. There was a lot going on in the Britain in August 1964. Virtually every Bank Holiday saw clashes between rival gangs of 'Mods' and 'Rockers.' 1964 also saw the abolition of the death penalty. Still on the theme of law and order, the year also saw appointment of the country's first black policeman. Increases in taxation quickly followed in an emergency budget designed to halt an unwelcome run on the pound.

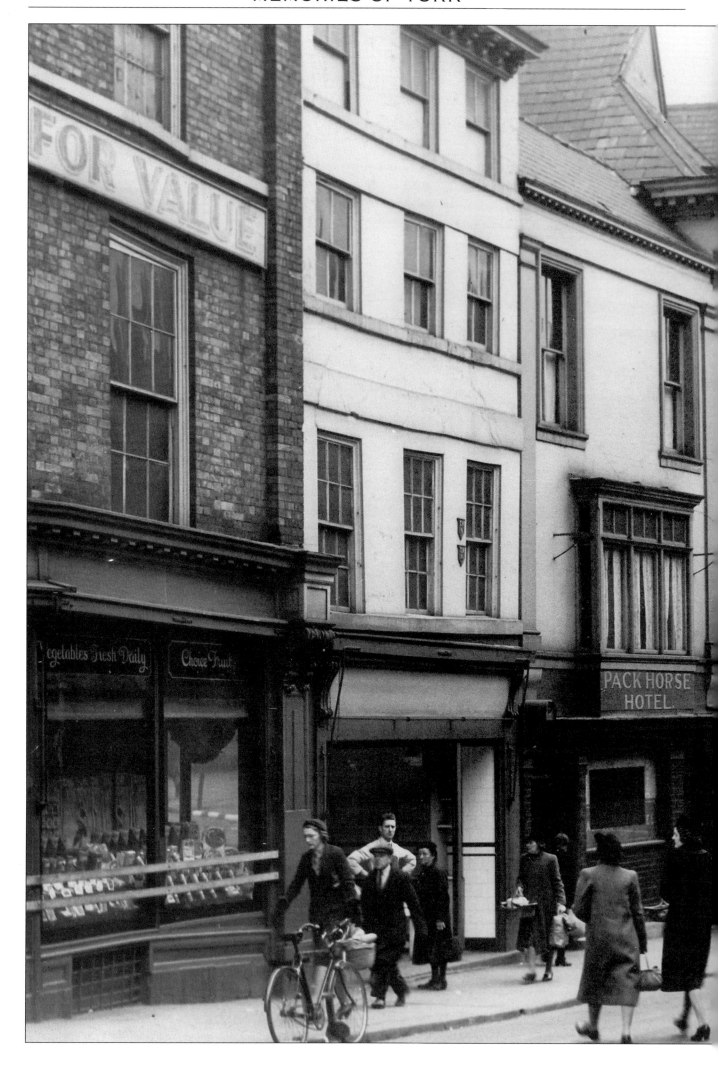

Located a short distance away from the modern premises it was later to occupy, the Co-operative store operated from numbers 6 to 14 Micklegate for many years. It can be seen here on the left of the photograph, next to the Argenta Meat Company, a butchers' shop. The butcher from the shop appears to be standing in front of his premises, hands on hips, staring at the camera and not looking too pleased at the prospect of having his picture taken! Number 20 Micklegate was the home of the Pack Horse Hotel which sold Hunt's Ebor Ales. Lower down the hill a rare view of the Adelphi Hotel (at number's 26 to 28) stood opposite the much larger Queen's Hotel. Some of the motorcars in the picture have blacked-out lamps, suggesting an early 1940s origin of the photograph.

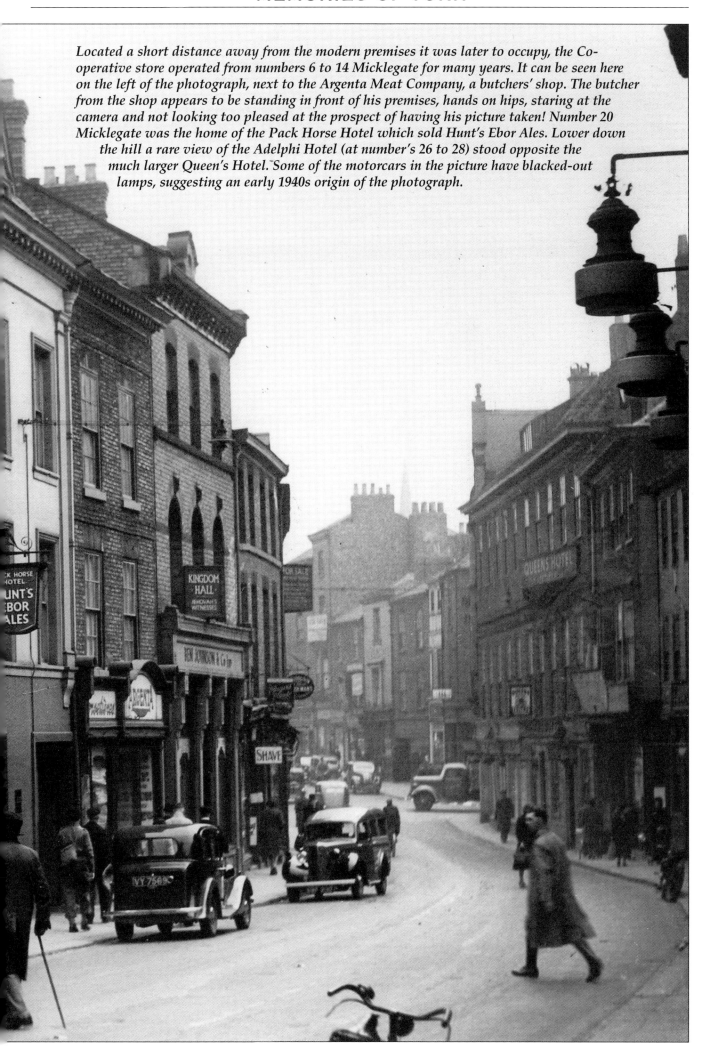

Below: *Olivers Furnishing Stores* offered a removal service as well as a range of affordable furniture which attracted people from all over the district to their Micklegate store. The location of the shop is marked in this picture by their distinctive square clock. On the left of the picture Shouksmiths ran their plumbing, glazing and ironmongers business from the property at number 128 -132, next to R. Trowedale's gents' hairdresser. Three public houses are shown in the picture; The Red Lion Hotel just right of Olivers and the Nags Head in the far distance. On the right of the picture the Coach and Horses, a Magnet house, can be seen beside the three cyclists approaching the camera. Evidence of wartime blackout precautions abound. The bumpers on the motorcars are painted white - a worthy but ineffective substitute for the car lamps which were shrouded so as not to attract the enemy bombers, and painted-out street lamps,

modified for the same reason. Readers may remember the 'one day boot repairers' on the left and N. Lumley's tobaconnists' shop next door.

Right: 'Buy now and save Purchase Tax' says the sign outside Waldenburgs' furniture shop. The bumper bars on the motors in the picture suggest a wartime date of origin. John Cross Ltd was next door to the popular Micklegate furnishers and many York folk may remember trips to the dentist located above it. Further down the street was the Cromwell Commercial Hotel with Cooper and Swan the Lithographers nearby. The Crown Hotel catered for thirsty drinkers - it was a good example of a no-frills city centre watering hole that existed long before anyone had thought up the idea of hideous theme pubs. Another public house, the Pack Horse stood opposite the 'Commercial.'

Below: A close-up view of a section of Micklegate which is believed to date from the 1940s. The picture concentrates upon two popular retail shops. The most imposing of these is the Williams Boot Repair Service, it may well be Mr Williams himself standing on the doorstep of the shop as the photograph is being taken. The signs at the shop make interesting reading. 'Ladies light shoes and gents' sewn footwear' reads one, and 'Repairs collected and delivered... only the best English leather used' proclaims another. The heavily shaded window next door belonged to R. Hanson, the Butcher. It would have been a full time job for him keeping out the heat of the summer sun - no refrigerators in those days of course, there was much reliance upon marble slabs and supplies of ice to keep the meat fresh.

> "BURTONS HAD SCORES OF OUTLETS THROUGHOUT BRITAIN, EACH WITH A REPUTATION FOR QUALITY AND GOOD VALUE"

The size of the Burtons empire was impressive - even half a century ago when this picture was taken. The York store can be seen just left of centre in this picture - it was one of scores of outlets created by Burtons throughout Britain, each with a distinctive white-faced facade and a reputation for quality and good value which was the envy of its many competitors. The smaller shop next door was the York home of Stead and Simpsons, part of another national chain, this one concerned with footwear. Those with sharp eyesight may be able to make out the two signs, one on each side of the street, indicating the location of the public air-raid shelter here on High Ousegate. Also featured here is the York Billiard Hall, again on the right, with Brown Brothers and Taylor the furnishers nearby. On the other side of the street, sadly out of view, the imposing structure of All Saints Church was located along with the Maypole Dairy and Boots the Chemists.

Above: Stonegate as it appeared in the 1950s - long before the age of pedestrianisation. This is one of the City's most ancient thoroughfares and the most ancient of hostelries, Ye Old Starre Inn (proprietor Mrs. Mary E. Smith) can be seen lower down the street near the Devonshire Tea Rooms. The distinctive sign has attracted thirsty customers to this spot for over a quarter of a *millennium!* At the time this picture was taken other businesses located along stonegate included the dressmakers known as 'Monique', Winifred Owen Gowns, 'Dinky' the dressmakers The Misses Cowper Dancing Academy and W. H Spink's Typewriters. Note the upright policeman walking smartly along the street on the right - complete with white gloves which would have given him additional authority as he carried out his patrol.

Right: Nostalgia abounds in this lovely old picture which dates from the 1940s. It features Fossgate, looking in the direction of Foss Islands Road. Three 'wartime' clues strike us immediately, each relating to the blackout regulations designed to make life difficult for the enemy bombers overhead; the lovely ornate lamp-standard on the right of the picture is painted white at the base in order to give drivers every chance of avoiding bumping into it. These drivers would have been travelling in cars with shrouded or blacked-out lights such as the one seen parked here - which provides us with the second clue to the date of the picture. Note too the painted-out bulb of the street lamp itself. As you might imagine, accidents increased tremendously in York (as elsewhere) during the blackout as cars crashed, pedestrians walked into lampposts and slipped off curbs. The government advised people to carry something white, or wear a white carnation... or leave their shirt tails out for added visibility!

You would have to be getting on in years to remember some of the shop names from this era; the Cash Clothing Company had just closed down (it is seen on the left of the picture on the edge of Lady Peckitts Yard); Albert Lee ran a gents outfitters' next door and must have been relieved when his competitor closed down, and the Blue Bell public house provided relief for thirsty drinkers a few doors down the street.

A slightly elevated view of the market, looking down Parliament Street of course, and showing the free passage of motorcars and motorcyles in the area before traffic was banished. The scene demonstrates just how popular the market area was - indeed, people would travel from the surrounding villages and many miles beyond them in order to experience the variety of bargains on offer at York market. Notice the British Road Service delivery van on the right of the picture. These olive green trucks were a familiar sight on the roads of virtually every town in the country in the 1950s and 60s when restrictions still applied to operation of many road hauliers, though not to the government-supported B.R.S organisation.

Above: A busy scene along Coney Street portrayed in this picture from 1966. A mixture of old and relatively new buildings, including The Mansion house, official home of the Lord Mayor of York, and Rowntrees Fashions, the Abbey National Building Society and the remains of St. Martin-le-Grand - the beautiful church which was badly damaged in the air-raids of April 1942. The most delightful clock in Yorkshire, attached to the church and now beautifully restored, looks out along Coney Street and can just be seen in this photograph, to the left of the Rowntrees store. Coney Street was once the location of York's local newspaper activities. York and County Press, publishers of the 'Evening Press' and the 'Gazette and Herald' owned a huge property on a riverside site which opened into Coney Street. They moved into purpose-built premises along Walmgate when the difficulties associated with inward and outward deliveries became overwhelming. To their credit the firm included a facility for environmentally-friendly river access to the new plant so that barges could deliver the dozens of huge rolls of newsprint that the plant consumes every day.

Right: A sunny August day in 1964 prompted a photographer to record this relaxed scene along Coney Street. The picture was taken from the south west. Leaders Fashions can be seen on the right of the picture, followed by the Singer Sewing Machine Shop, Crockatts Cleaners and the Westminster Bank. Those with keen eyesight, or long memories, may be able to fix the location of 'Cantors' further along Coney Street, shown here with a 'nostalgic' Standard Eight saloon car driving past it. Citizens often resist the moves towards pedestrianisation in our retail centres and the notion that people and cars simply don't mix. Some of the pictures contained in this book make a mockery of that point of view, and the move into York's pedestrian era should be applauded.

Toyshop on television

Albert London's business was set up in 1914. He had been a coach painter, but, after his son Fred had lost the fingers of one hand whilst working as a butcher, Albert thought a newsagency would be a way of earning a living for Fred where a damaged hand would not be too much of a disadvantage.

The first shop was at 20 East Parade and business prospered. Unfortunately Fred passed away suddenly at an early age but his wife and two of his sisters joined the business. All the family performed all necessary tasks as required, with the help of the usual team of boys to do the morning and evening deliveries.

In 1931 a move was made to the corner of Mill Lane, Heworth. As well as newspapers and magazines the shop sold a wide range of related goods including stationery and paper goods, tobacco and tobacco products and toys.

When the family lived in Millington House a shop was built extending from Millington House round Mill Lane Corner. A further extension to enlarge the business was put up in 1984. The present shop is very

large and on two floors. A large range of confectionery has been added to the stock. The personal customer service means the business still prospers in spite of competition from such large concerns as Argos and Toys R Us.

The shop's reputation for being customer-friendly led, recently, to an invitation to take part in a television programme. Children had written in to the BBC complaining that Newsagents shops discouraged children from coming in and looking round. Londons were chosen for a programme which featured a busload of children arriving at the shop and wandering around at their leisure. Such public confirmation of Londons' care for their customers can only mean even more success in the future.

Above: An early advertisement for the newsagency.
Below: Fred London and his delivery bike outside the shop during the first World War.

The family with the bright ideas

By July 1897 George Barnitt was flourishing as a 'General and Furnishing Ironmonger and Agricultural Implement Agent' at 24, Colliergate, York. The Retail Trades' Review thoroughly recommended him. "Repairs of all kinds are undertaken, while the prices charged are strictly moderate. This business is under practical management in every department."

George came from farming stock and so felt at home selling agricultural ironmongery and could give his customers sound practical advice. After a while he took on an apprentice, Edwin Thompson (the present Mr Thompson's uncle).

Having served his apprenticeship, Edwin left to gain wider experience working with a relative, Ernest Thompson, in Leeds. When he heard that George Barnitt wanted to sell his business in Colliergate, Edwin came back to York to buy and run it. He had the company incorporated in 1913, when it became Barnitts Ltd. There was not enough work at this point for two men and so Ernest remained in Leeds until war broke out in 1939. Then, when the young men in the firm went into the armed forces, Ernest came to York. His bad health had prevented his call up but he became a proficient director of the business.

Ernest's son Ian joined the business when he left school in 1955. Ian served his apprenticeship in the family business, then left to learn more from employment with a similar but much larger company when he was twenty. Quite soon he was back working in Colliergate as neither Edwin nor his father was well enough to run the family business. Ian became a director of Barnitts when Ernest Thompson died in 1962. Edwin lived for a further five years before he died of cancer in 1967. In that year, Ian Thompson became Chairman and Managing Director of the family firm having

managed the business since the age of 21. Over the years, Edwin had bought 26, Colliergate and had begun to design and manufacture the firm's own brand of fireplaces, "Barnitts". In the fifties three more properties and a yard were acquired. One shop had belonged to a florist and another to a milliner and all the properties adjoined the original. They were all made into one connecting store.

As the store grew it began to offer a much wider range of stock including ironmongery, hardware, electrical appliances, power tools and a large gardening department selling everything from seeds to garden furniture. The shop continued to expand, building over the car park it had purchased at the rear of the store and can now offer everything for the home from fine glassware and china, crockery, bathroom fittings and mirrors to pine furniture. There is also a superb soft furnishings and wallpaper department stocking a wide range of exclusive and popular designs. All this variety has led to the local saying "If Barnitts haven't got it, you can't get it anywhere!"

Four years ago the company bought the Territorial Drill Hall at 28 Colliergate and 60% of this has now been converted, adding a further 17,000 square feet of showroom space to Barnitts with the remainder due for completion by the end of 1998. Presently it employs a staff of 72 including part-timers, a vast difference from the early days when the young Edwin Thompson was serving his apprenticeship. The firm is still very much a family concern, Ian Thompson's son Paul and his daughter Sally are now in the business and the current Directors besides Ian are his wife, Maureen, his sister Pat and his son Paul.

Top: The Colliergate premises at the turn of the century.
Centre: The same premises seen in the 1970s.
Left: A 1920s advertisement for the company's products.

Mulberry Hall: the jewel of York

Mulberry Hall, situated in Stonegate, one of York's narrow Roman streets, is one of the world's leading fine china and crystal specialists. Its beautifully preserved medieval building, dating from 1434 with its splendid Tudor frontage is just 200 yards from York Minster and is a most appropriate setting for the very finest displays of porcelain and crystal.

During the 15th Century the building was a private house and was once the residence of the Bishop of Chester. It became a shop in the 18th Century.

Mulberry Hall was established in 1962 by Michael Sinclair whose family had a separate china and crystal business in Doncaster. Beauty and quality were his by-words which made for high overheads.

Having bought the most exclusive and delicately made stock, he needed to display it in a setting that did it justice. Having chosen just the right building (where the business rates are crippling!) he needed to provide superb shop fittings. As he said, "Everything about Mulberry Hall costs the most."

Consequently, for Mulberry Hall's customers, a visit is not only a shopping trip but an entry into a magical world where nothing is other than delightful.

The shop comprises seventeen showrooms and is the largest of its kind in the United Kingdom. In 1994 its new Royal Copenhagen and Georg Jensen room was opened by Her Royal Highness the Duchess of Gloucester. Over the years the Mulberry Hall name has spread nationally and internationally through its mail order and bridal services. It is now internationally recognised as the leading mail order specialist in its field.

Apart from mail order trade, most of Mulberry Hall's custom comes from people who live within a 100 mile radius of York. Merchandise is exported as far afield as the USA, Japan, Korea, China, Australia and New Zealand. The company's packers are experts, as customers would expect, and the goods they despatch to all parts of the world are fully insured.

Mulberry Hall is proud of the high standards it maintains and the fact that it is considered to be one of the best shops in Europe for fine china and crystal. Its unsurpassed stock includes English bone china by Wedgwood, Royal Worcester, Spode, Minton, Royal Doulton and Royal Crown Derby; porcelain by Royal Copenhagen, Herend and Meissen; crystal by Waterford, Stuart, Baccarat, Moser, Daum, William Yeoward and Lalique; enamels by Halcyon Days and silver by Georg Jensen.

For further information you can browse the Mulberry Hall web pages on www.mulberryhall.co.uk

Above: A fine line drawing of the Tudor frontage of Mulberry Hall. *Opposite page:* Mulberry Hall on Stonegate pictured at the turn of the century. *Below:* The exterior of Mulberry Hall as it is today, beautifully maintained as befits such an exclusive store.

Left: A rare view of Pavement which dates from the 1940s and contains many interesting features. To the modern eye the first impression is just how much the street has changed since the picture was taken. This row of properties looks out on one of the most historic areas of York and is now substantially renovated. 'Pavement' is a name which reflects the fact that this was the first street in York to be paved. Note the anonymous-looking grey property (with twin gables) to the left of T. Coning and Sons; it is the former house of Sir Thomas Herbert. The sixteenth-century facade is now substantially restored to the bright black and white appearance that tourists admire today. Conings, already mentioned, were tea and coffee merchants. Lloyds Bank had a branch on the right of the picture, next to Kent and Brydon the seed and bulb merchants. Within striding distance were some of the busiest stores in York, including British Home Stores, Currys (who began as cycle and radio dealers), and, of course Marks and Spencer. Other premises in this area were occupied by Avon Insurance, the National Farmers Union offices and York Coffee House Company.

Below: The sunshades were out along Micklegate when this picture was taken. It is thought to date from the 1950s, a couple of clues being the motorcars at the top-left of the picture, one being a Morris Minor and the other a Morris Oxford pick-up. Just right of centre, at number 56 Micklegate, the baby linen shop owned by Mrs. Muriel Lyon can be seen. Hundreds of readers will no doubt remember trips for gifts and supplies for new babies to Mrs. Lyons' shop. The flower shop at number 60 Micklegate was known as *Bouquets by Beryl*; George Woodcock ran the baker and confectioners further along the street.

Above: More modern times are represented by this photograph which dates from 1980. It was taken in the month of June and features the 'new-look' Parliament Street. The department store premises going under the name of W.P Brown Ltd can be seen in the background. The canopy of the North East Electricity Board juts out over the pavement on the top left of the picture and runs parallel to the row of modern, though now slightly dated motors parked on the side of the street. Across that street Maynards can be seen beside the Scholl shop and John Colliers the gents' tailors. The picture would not be complete without a piece of 'old York' peeping out over the scene and the Gothic beauty of the Mister is visible in the distance.

Top right: A mixture of architectural styles, some original and others quite dramatic in appearance. In the centre of the picture the Lendal Bridge Inn can be seen with the Spink Typewriter Company to the left of it. Spinks' had branches in Leeds, Bradford and Wakefield. Another commercial property of note in this area was the Pickfords removal depot, seen beneath the elaborate sign which reads 'Horse and Carriage Repository and Commission Stables.' The building had been shortened considerably since it was built in 1884 and had the distinction of being called one of the ugliest buildings in Europe. Also located on Rougier Street was Central Garage (the Vauxhall and Bedford dealers) and the off licence which was owned by Sidney Smith for many years. In later years the appearance of this area would be transformed by the construction of the General Accident offices.

Right: This section of Goodramgate was photographed in 1963. The section of housing known as Lady Row is said to be the oldest block of domestic housing in the city, dating back over 400 years. The picture was taken in December 1963, shortly before the onset of a terrible winter which brought much of the country to a grinding halt. The picture was taken from the south east and the row of damp cars, including an Austin A40, a Ford Cortina and a Riley '1500' serve to add a sense of character to the scene.

Notice too the motorcycle combination squeezed in between the Ford and the Austin. It would have provided the occupants with a bumpy, uncertain

HAMMONDS ALES

LENDAL BRIDGE INN

PICKFORDS
REMOVAL ENQUIRY OFFICE

but economical ride in its day. This small patch of land would later be the site of a row of modern shops. Some of the shop names along Lady Row might bring back a memory or two; Ye Olde Biscuit Shop, the Clothes Hospital (well known for speedy alterations to any garment you can mention) with Lidsters' to the right of it.

Freshly cut flowers have always been a speciality at the open market and this photograph, dating from around 1960, shows an attractive setting near one of the popular flower stalls. Two stalwarts of national retailing, Marks and Spencers and British Home Stores can be seen at the side of the market area - they have played, and continue to play a leading role in the retailing activities of York, attracting visitors from home and abroad to the city as well as providing jobs and serving the needs of her local residents.

Sporting life

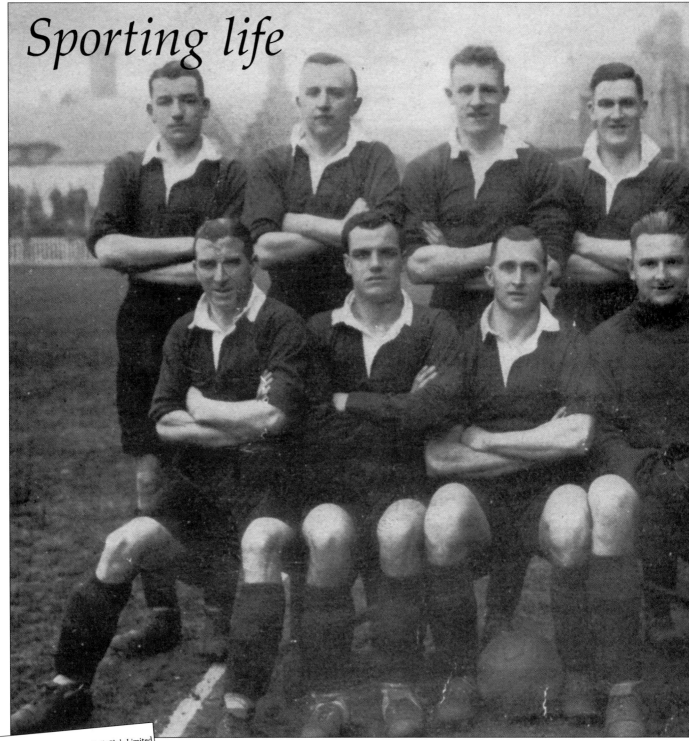

The Sheffield Wednesday Football Club Limited

Complimentary Luncheon

to

YORK CITY F.C.

and

NEWCASTLE UNITED F.C.

GRAND HOTEL, SHEFFIELD
SATURDAY, 26th MARCH, 1955

Above: This first team York City squad for the 1937/8 season is featured in this postcard souvenir from that time. The reverse of the card carries a wealth of information relating to the team, including the players names. The back row of this group featured P. Spooner, E. Wass, R. Baines, C. Barrett, E. Hathaway, J. Hughes and T. Lockie (Trainer). On the front row we see M. Comrie, S. Earl, R. Duckworth (Captain), N. Wharton and J. Pinder.

A further note on the postcard describes how the team played in 'old gold and black' for the only time for their clash with West Bromwich Albion in the 4th Round of the F.A Cup. During this cup run York City went to the 6th Round where they drew 0-0 with Huddersfield before losing by two goals to one in the replay.

Left: A delightful piece of football nostalgia in the form of a menu from the complimentary luncheon hosted by Sheffield Wednesday Football Club on Saturday 26 March 1955 at the Grand Hotel in Sheffield. A toast to the visitors proposed by Colonel R.L Craig O.B.E of the Sheffield club. It would have been an unforgettable occasion for the players and staff from York.

Top right: A shilling would have bought this Happy Wanderers football souvenir when it was published in 1955. It would cost much more than that if you wanted to buy one now of course. In a welcoming foreword section in the book the Chairman, Hugh Kitchen, spoke of the honour and the glory that had been brought to the club and the City of York by Ernest Phillips and the players.

Right: The official programme for the 1955 Challenge Cup semi-final tie between York City and Newcastle United at Hillsborough. York City was only the second Northern Section club to have reached the semi-final. They had reached the 'last eight' in the cup in the 1938 season when they were beaten by Huddersfield Town in the replay. The 1955 squad was made up of a combination of full and part-time players. York's team consisted of Tommy Forgan, Ernest Phillips, George Howe, Gordon Brown, Alan Stewart, Ron Spence, William Hughes, Arthur Bottom, Norman Wilkinson, Sidney Storey and William Fenton.

At work

Above: This 1950s view of workers arriving by bus at the Rowntrees factory is a far cry from the very humble beginnings of the business when it operated out of a small shop along Pavement. As you might expect, the workers in this picture are overwhelmingly female, and it is interesting to note that this was the era of the headscarf and the turban as far as headgear was concerned.

The style of the building is decidedly utilitarian, save for the large columns and massive stone blocks used to create this rather intimidating entrance. York's confectionery industry has served the City well over a period of around a century, providing worthwhile employment opportunities and boosting the image of the area throughout the world.

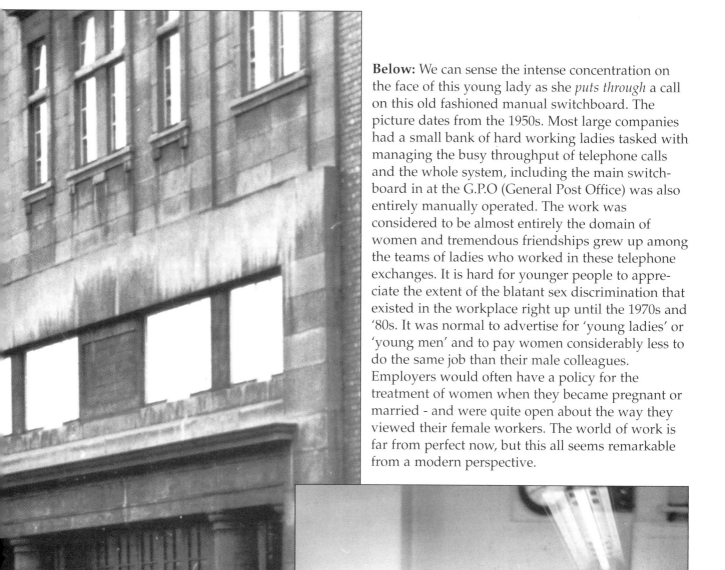

Below: We can sense the intense concentration on the face of this young lady as she *puts through* a call on this old fashioned manual switchboard. The picture dates from the 1950s. Most large companies had a small bank of hard working ladies tasked with managing the busy throughput of telephone calls and the whole system, including the main switchboard in at the G.P.O (General Post Office) was also entirely manually operated. The work was considered to be almost entirely the domain of women and tremendous friendships grew up among the teams of ladies who worked in these telephone exchanges. It is hard for younger people to appreciate the extent of the blatant sex discrimination that existed in the workplace right up until the 1970s and '80s. It was normal to advertise for 'young ladies' or 'young men' and to pay women considerably less to do the same job than their male colleagues. Employers would often have a policy for the treatment of women when they became pregnant or married - and were quite open about the way they viewed their female workers. The world of work is far from perfect now, but this all seems remarkable from a modern perspective.

Below: Rougier Street in a view taken looking towards the north east of the city. The area was about to be transformed by the construction of the huge office complex which was to be the regional headquarters of a well-known insurance firm. York has been luckier than most cities, for fairly obvious reasons, in as much as it did not suffer too greatly in the 1960s and '70s from the rush to rip out the commercial heart of the area and replace it with concrete shopping malls and multi-story car parks. Of course, there are exceptions, but the planners should be given credit for achieving a balance between the practical needs of modern shoppers, residents and tourists, and the major responsibility of maintaining the character and fabric of the area for future generations.

Very few historic cities have achieved the elusive blend of 'originality' and 'practicality' with the same effect as York.

> **"ROWNTREES PROVIDED EMPLOYMENT FOR WHOLE FAMILIES IN THE CITY AND FOR THOUSANDS OF PEOPLE OVER THE YEARS."**

Right: A familiar sight to the thousands of people who have worked at Rowntrees over the years and remember walking in and out of this entrance of the factory. The distinctive clock shows that the photograph was taken a little after 12.30 p.m, suggesting that the workers are leaving the site for their lunchtime break. *Rowntrees* provided employment for whole families in the City and, along with other well-known confectioners, helped to make 'York' famous throughout many continents. The benevolence of the Rowntree family in various forms (not least of which being the donation to the citizens of York of Rowntree Park) has characterised the organisation over many decades.

Nestlé - making a necessity out of a luxury

The history of Nestlé spans almost three centuries and has the origins of three companies which have combined to make it one of the world leaders in confectionery today.

The York connection

Mary Tuke, a Quaker who lived in York opened a grocer's shop in the heart of the City in 1725. By 1785 the shop was being run by her family, trading under the name of William Tuke & Sons. One of the products they sold was cocoa and by 1815 the company had begun to manufacture its own chocolate.

In 1862 Henry Isaac Rowntree acquired the cocoa and chocolate side of the business which was quickly expanded. Henry's brother Joseph became his partner in 1869 and the company was re-named H.I. Rowntree & Co.

The company manufactured a large range of cocoas, including 'Rock Cocoa', which was a fine blend of cocoa and sugar, sold in blocks. At that time they also introduced Chocolate Drops and Creams, and Penny and Half Penny Cream Balls.

With the introduction of Fruit Gums and Fruit Pastilles in the early 1880s, there came the need to expand and they bought and converted a flour mill, the site of the

Above: Henry Rowntree pictured in 1870. Below: Chocolate packing in 1910, in the York premises at Haxby Road.

York factory today, buying the 141 acre site a few years later. Sadly in 1883 Henry died, leaving Joseph in sole control.

In 1897 the firm was established as a limited company with Joseph as Chairman with his son, Benjamin Seebohm joining the company. Seebohm took over his father as Chairman in 1923 and Joseph died two years later.

Paternal policy

The Rowntrees were strict Quakers and set up business as chocolate manufacturers as it was deemed acceptable for them to do so, because chocolate was seen as a product that spread happiness with health-giving benefits. Joseph Rowntree was frustrated that he couldn't deploy his Quaker principles for the benefit of his workforce. In 1904 the Joseph Rowntree village was set up and in the next few years the company intro-duced schemes to benefit their workers including a widow's benefit fund, a workers' dining room and a gymnasium and the appointment

Above: The development of KitKat, introduced in the 1930s and originally known as Chocolate Crisp. Closer inspection reveals a packet which was issued during the rationing of the 1940s and early 50s. Plain chocolate was used as there was such a shortage of milk.

Top: Another view of the chocolate packing department at Haxby Road, York.

of an optician. The company also gave workers an annual weeks paid holiday and by 1919 the working week was reduced to forty four hours. In 1902 Joseph, concerned that he could no longer know every member of staff personally, launched the staff magazine and wrote in the first edition "The increasing number of those who are associated with the Cocoa Works - more than 2000 - makes it impossible to keep up a personal acquaintance with the staff as fully as was the case in the earlier years of the business. I hope this periodical may to some extent make up for the loss of personal intercourse that has thus been occasioned."

Following Seebohm's succession as Chairman, the company expanded rapidly introducing more and more ranges to their brand, Black Magic chocolates in 1933, Kit-Kat and Aero in 1935,

Left: *Packing Dairy Box in the 1950s.*
Below: *The scale of the factory at Haxby Road is evident in this 1950s picture. The girl in the centre of the picture seems to find the whole idea of the photograph quite amusing.*

Dairy Box in 1936, Smarties in 1937, Polo Mints in 1948, After Eight in 1962 and Matchmakers in 1968 - all of which are familiar faces, even in todays overcrowded market.

George Harris became Chairman in 1941. Prior to this, as marketing director he had been responsible for introducing new brands during the 1930s and 1940s. Sadly Seebohm Rowntree died in 1954.

The mergers

Rowntree and Mackintosh joined forces in 1969, being renamed as Rowntree Mackintosh and in 1988 the company joined Swiss-owned Nestlé SA for £2.5 billion, becoming the Nestlé Rowntree division of Nestlé UK Ltd.

1989 was a time for change for the company. Peter Blackburn was appointed Chairman of Rowntree Mackintosh and at the same time Nestlé's confectionery business was transferred to York and for the first time, Nestlé's shares were quoted on the London Stock Exchange. In 1991 Peter Blackburn was appointed Chairman and Managing Director of Nestlé Holdings UK Ltd, combining the Nestlé and Rowntree Mackintosh businesses in the UK.

In 1992 a new Polo Mint plant was built in York, with the addition of a chocolate making plant a year later and a two finger KitKat factory in 1994.

Expansion and growth are constantly in the forefront of the company's collective mind and in 1994 a Group and Regional Laboratory, costing over £1.5 million, opened in York. The Group also won the Queen's Award for Export Achievement during the same year (the company's exports account for 28% of all production). With a history that spans 280 years from England to Switzerland, the Group is confident that its future will be just as successful.

Above: Smarties, first introduced in 1937 and still very popular today. It is interesting to note how the packaging has developed to cater for the more discerning youngsters of today. Top: A 1950s picture showing a trainee being taught the fine art of hand-piping chocolates.

From brewing ale to leadworking excellence

The marriage of Jonas Shouksmith of Bradford to Mary Plummer in Micklegate in 1787 provided him not only with a wife but also a new home. He was a brewer by his trade which he followed for several years, living in Tanner Row. In 1806 he purchased his freemanship of the City of York, describing himself as an 'ale-draper' who was obviously selling his own brew.

In 1822 Joseph Richard advertised in the City of York Directory, calling himself 'Plumber and Glazier' trading from St Mary's Row, Bishophill. He married John Jackson's daughter, Hannah, and their elder son, Thomas, joined the business. Thomas died in 1861 leaving six young children and a widow, Ann, who took responsibility for the business until her death in 1864. Joseph Richard again took up the reins until his death in 1866 when two of his grandsons, Joseph and John Henry, continued the business until the latter bought it in 1878 giving it its present name J H Shouksmith. Meanwhile Thomas's other sons established businesses in Fairfax Street and Blossom Street, York.

In 1872, John Henry married Julia Mary North whose father was manager of the York Union Banking Company. They had five children and their two sons, Thomas Henry and Arthur William, went to work with their father.

The Shouksmith family have a long

His second son, Joseph Richard turned his back on brewing and was apprenticed to John Jackson, a plumber. He became a Master Craftsman but had to become a Freeman too before he was allowed to employ workmen. When he became a Freeman of the City in 1820 he established the company which exists to this day.

Above: Thomas Henry Shouksmith 1873 - 1969.
Right: The beautiful, hand-painted certificate presented to Thomas Henry, on the occasion of 75 years with the company, by his co-directors and staff of the firm.

connection with Micklegate, moving into number 59 (now number 128) in 1824.

In 1913 John Henry Shouksmith took the first of two radical steps in the company's history, formalising a deed of partnership with his two sons Thomas and Arthur. In 1919 Shouksmiths became a limited liability company, one of the first in York. When John Henry died in 1924, his elder son, Thomas, became Chairman and with his brother Arthur, ran the company for many years. At the age of 90 Thomas was presented with a service certificate celebrating 75 years with the company and both he and Arthur continued taking an active interest until their deaths in 1969 and 1968 respectively when their service to the company had lasted for 81 and 73 years. Thomas had no children but Arthur's elder son William Henry (known as Harry) Shouksmith became Chairman and his younger brother Philip Harold joined the business. Harry was largely responsible for expanding the business in the era following the Second World War when building was at its peak. On the death of William Henry, his nephews Colin Maxwell Foster, Philip Harold's

Above: The rear of the Micklegate premises in 1902.
Below: An example of a classical lead rainwater head and pipe for restoration work in the 1950s.

son, Richard Philip Shouksmith took over the running of the business in 1987 and are still in charge today. In all there have been six generations of Shouksmiths, all Freemen of the City of York.

The growth of the company since the end of the Second World War has been affected by the effects of recession but it has grown into a group of companies covering most of England. It has diversified into lead work,

industrial heating and air conditioning, property owning and development in addition to the original plumbing work.

The Shouksmith group has divisions in York, Leeds, Gloucester and Worksop. From Leeds it carries out industrial and commercial heating, ventilation and air conditioning throughout the UK. From the other premises it concentrates on plumbing work including drainage, rainwater systems, hot and cold services, sanitation and gas, all types of building and domestic heating including sheltered accommodation.

Top: Directors of the company in 1963, from left; brothers Arthur William Shouksmith and Thomas Henry Shouksmith and William Henry Shouksmith, son of Arthur William. **Above:** *Copper orb and cross pinnacle to sheet copper Church roof covering, 1960s.* **Right:** *David Dutton and Charlie Mitchell relaying the lead on the roof of All Saints Church, Coppergate in 1944.*

It is a major specialist in lead, copper and stainless steel sheet roofing. For all these services it provides full design facilities as required.

Throughout its history, the company has done work on many notable buildings but none gave more pleasure than the contract to replace the copper roof on the North Transept to York Minster with lead in 1989. The company believes that the high reputation that it enjoys is confirmed by the majority of its work being repeat business. Its commitment to its staff is demonstrated by its having presented over 140 gold watches for long service. If Jonas Shouksmith could have seen into the future of his marriage to Mary Plummer more than 200 years ago, he might have been greatly surprised to see how many of his descendants still live in York. He would have been proud to know that the firm founded by his son and now a diversified group of companies, still continues to offer traditional plumbing work to a standard of which he would have approved.

Top left: *The new lead roof on the North Transept of York Minster laid by the company in 1989.* **Top right:** *Sheet copper roof for an 18th Century ice house, covered in 1995.* **Above:** *The Craftsmanship Award presented to Maurice Clarkson of J H Shouksmith & Sons, commended for his craftsmanship as a leadworker.*
Left: *Sheet leadwork in progress to the roof apex during construction of the new General Accident building in York 1995.*

In the great tradition of Medieval Craftsmen

Dick Reid's studio and workshop in Fishergate, follow the great tradition of decorative craftsmanship in York from medieval times when all the Craft Guilds were represented here, through the great flowering of carving in the 17th and 18th centuries, to the 1950s when the plain facades of modernism came in.

Dick Reid arrived in York by chance - sent by the Army in 1956 as a National Service Officer for three years. Having served his time in Newcastle under Ralph Hedley as an architectural Wood and Stone Carver, he decided to settle in York to build his business. Forced to teach through lack of demand, at the Manor School, then in Priory Street, he demonstrated his skills in a tiny studio on a 3rd floor in Stonegate and began to lecture to local interest groups as a form of advertising. With the growth in national wealth in the mid 1960s the restoration of the great country houses resumed and demand for carving skills returned. In 1965 the workshop moved to Grape Lane and a lifelong association with the architect Francis Johnson through an introduction by William Anelay, began. This led to many restoration projects including Heath Hall, Wakefield and Everingham Park near Beverley and in

recent years the making of fine furniture for British Embassies round the world. The patronage of Bernard Johnson of Ben Johnsons Printers, led to heraldic carving commissions in the Guild Halls of the Taylors Company and Merchant Adventurers. Church and Cathedral work began to come in with the encouragement of the Dean of York, Eric Milner-White, who had recognised his skills.

With the move to a larger workshop commissions expanded to include cabinet making and antique restoration and the employment of other craftsmen. The quality of work was recognised by the Master Carvers' Association which has since elected Dick Reid their President twice, and an invitation to join Craft Committees both in London and Scotland. The high standard of craftsmanship achieved by 'in house' apprentice training led to the involvement of the workshop in the major

Top right: The clay model for the plaster casting bound for Chatelherault in Scotland.
Top left: A detail of a carved oak seat in the Gothic style for Ashridge College. *Centre:* Incised lettering in Purbeck Marble with bronze inset at Westminster Abbey. *Right:* A statuary marble chimney piece from the Palm Room in Spencer House, London.

GEORGE GREEN MATHEMATICIAN & PHYSICIST -1793- 1841

restoration of Fairfax House for the York Civic Trust and at Chatelherault in Hamilton, Scotland; both involving stone and wood carving and modelling by a team of seven craftsmen and women.

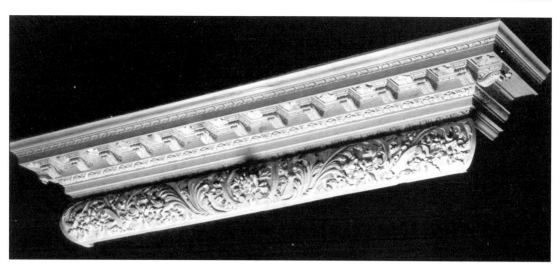

By 1989 a core team of ten had been trained which could tackle carving, modelling, letter cutting,

gilding and turning. With this expansion and the introduction of pedestri-anisation in York city centre, the workshop was moved to its present location 'without' the City wall in Fishergate. Since then the team has had a major input into the restoration of Spencer House in London for Lord Rothschild, which demanded excellence in the replication of finely carved furniture and architectural elements in wood and five major chimneypieces in marble over a period of four years. Work has also included the making and restoration of furniture for the Historic Royal Palaces Agency at Kensington Palace and Hampton Court and the refurbishment of Hertford House for the Wallace Collection. The workshop also undertakes the designing, cutting and illumi-nating of lettering for major memorials in many Cathedrals and churches including Westminster Abbey.

More recently the workshop has been involved with the restoration of Windsor Castle after the fire, where Dick Reid was appointed to supervise the restoration of the Carlton House Trophies. Newly designed work has also been undertaken in the US and Ireland. Dick Reid himself has been a Trustee of the Prince of Wales's Institute of Architecture, where

he also lectures. He is a regular lecturer at other institutions and his dream of estab-lishing a multi-skilled workforce on the Renaissance workshop pattern has been fulfilled.

Top: A carved overdoor in pine at Fairfax House in York. Centre: A detail from a part finished marble carving at Spencer House in London. Left: Craftsmen at work in Dick Reid's busy studio.

Garbutt and Elliott - personal and caring service to the people of York

The renowned York Chartered Accountancy firm, Garbutt and Elliott, was founded in 1884 by Mr Pearson, in offices at Judges Court, off Coney Street and was originally known as Pearson and Taylor. This was in the days of quill pens, lots of coloured inks, blotting paper and ready reckoners.

The business ran its own building society, the York Permanent Benevolent Building Society; which operated from the same offices until it was wound up in 1949. Indeed, the offices were set out more as a building society than an accountants office and had an enormous built-in safe that has had to remain with the building until the present day.

The firm became O.G. Taylor and Garbutt at the beginning of the thirties and shortly afterwards Mr Elliott Snr joined the office on January 1st 1935. The onset of war in 1939 put his partnership prospects on hold and during the war he and Mr Ernest Brown, who worked for the firm for 50 years, did the accountancy work whilst Mr Garbutt was in charge of the Home Guard in York and was visited by army personnel most days. Not content with this day-time involvement in the war Mr Garbutt was also an air-raid warden during the evenings!

The offices at Judges Court were reputedly haunted and whilst Mr Elliott Snr and Mr Brown were working one evening on the first floor, they heard footsteps on the stairs. Both came out of their offices to greet the visitor but no-one was there! According to one of the local "Ghost Walks" it is the ghost of a soldier killed in the building during the 18th Century.

Mr Elliott Snr, achieved his goal of being a partner in 1947 and the name of the firm became W.D. Garbutt and Elliott, and apart from dropping Mr Garbutt's

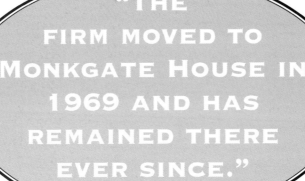

> "THE FIRM MOVED TO MONKGATE HOUSE IN 1969 AND HAS REMAINED THERE EVER SINCE."

initials, the name has remained unchanged for more than 50 years.

Sadly, Mr Garbutt died in 1949 leaving Mr Elliott Snr as sole practitioner. The business grew steadily despite losing substantial utility clients due to nationalisation, including the Market Weighton Drainage Board, The County Hospital and Bootham Park Hospital, although they continued to act for the York Waterworks Company.

In 1960, after 76 years at the Judges Court, the firm leased the Red House, Duncombe Place from the City Council, and in 1964 Mr Elliott's son, Bob, became a partner together with Les King. When articled clerk (now partner) Colin Foster went through the floorboards during one of the regular games of football in the office, it was felt that it was time to move and to buy premises rather than to lease.

The partners purchased Monkgate House in 1969. It had formerly been the home of George Hudson "the Railway King" but it was almost derelict and Mr Elliott Snr even had to get a personal loan from his sister in Southend to enable them to do the necessary renovations. The move to Monkgate was, with hindsight, a very wise decision, because by moving from the city centre to just outside the Bar walls Garbutt and Elliott have the best of both worlds - a few minutes by foot from the city centre, yet with lots of parking which nowadays is a rare commodity in York. Many businesses have followed suit over recent years.

With the onset of computers, E-mail and fax machines, accounts and tax return preparation is far

different from the early days. Garbutt and Elliott offer a one-stop business advisory, tax and financial planning service to owner managed businesses, professional partnerships and private clients from throughout the country, but especially around Yorkshire. They give a very personal and approachable service to their clients, look to build up long term relationships, and offer a high level of technical expertise.

Looking to the future Garbutt and Elliott want to continue to develop their services and further increase their level of specialist expertise in order to be able to provide a complete service to all their clients, while still offering the personal and caring service that has long been their trademark.

Above: The firm's offices at Monkgate House. Facing page: Red House, Duncombe Place, home of the firm from 1960 to 1969. Left: A professional team of experts, who are well equipped to deal with all situations.

More than just messing about on the river

Yacht Service Limited began life at Naburn immediately after the Second World War - on 8th June 1945. The site had previously been used as a pontoon bridging school by the Army.

After a few precarious years, as peoples lives became more normal, the business began to grow slowly, and to offer more facilities on the River Ouse.

1959 was the first breakthrough year, as there was more leisure time and money around so interest in personal boating began to grow. At first the concentration was on outboard motors, very small boats or dinghies with a selection of boat fittings and equipment.

By 1963 it was decided to extend the repair side of the business to include new cruisers which were timber built throughout in those days. Dania, pictured opposite was constructed in 1961 and was the first boat to be built at Naburn. Business was expanded later to include the fitting out of fibreglass hulls to an extremely high standard.

As the interest in boating grew, so the need for somewhere to moor ones boat became a priority too. In 1967 a small marina covering a three acre site was excavated alongside the River Ouse, with facilities for 100 pleasure craft.

By 1970 the demand for new craft had grown to such an extent that a small 'custom' boat building firm was unable to satisfy the need, so it was

Above: Bringing a boat in from the river, 1947.
Below: Launching a pleasure craft into the river, 1962.

decided to take on Agencies to cover a range from 18 ft to 34 ft luxury cruisers from national manufacturers. These were the boom years, when the Marina was expanded to cover its present 18 acres, and the latest self-propelled hydraulic boat lift was installed to enable boats to be moved to any part of the property.

The business now concentrates on larger luxury craft up to £250,000.00, but still retains its original base for repairs and maintenance to all makes of craft, boat fittings and equipment, and dry storage space during the winter months, and all year berthing facilities in the Marina. Although Naburn

Top and above: The pleasure craft 'Dania' being built during 1961 and afloat following her launch in 1962.
Left: Celebrating the launch of 'Dania', from left to right; Mrs Pool, Allan, Tom, Tony, Andrew, Frank, Mr Pool, Jimmy, Willy, Bob and Mrs Thompson with Janet and Alan in front.

is an inland Marina, there is a much wider cruising area within easy reach. The River Ouse extends to the River Humber which leads to the River Trent, the canal system of the country, the East Coast and even further afield.

As Sealine York the company are distributors of the Sealine range of luxury cruisers in the North of England, from the Senator series, a two to four berth trailable Sports cruiser, ranging from an 8 metre boat for family cruising and water sports, to a mid range 11 metre open cockpit cruiser offering four to seven berths, all with a wide range of single and twin engine options for economy or performance.

The even larger Statesman, up to 16 metres, is the height of luxury with a variety of aft cabin layouts to suit different needs, giving six to eight berth accommodation and a wide choice of engine installations.

Leisure time is precious, and the company is committed to ensure that their customers get full enjoyment from their Sealine luxury cruiser, whether it is starting out with a trailable Senator or moving up into the dignified elegance of a Statesman.

The company's experience and attention to detail will help their customers to derive the greatest pleasure from their choice of a Sealine cruiser.

From a small local firm, covering the North East, the business has expanded Nationwide with representation at the International Boat Shows in the country.

Top: A well used marina as it appeared in 1980. Above: The family sports cruiser, a Sealine Senator 240 offering four berth accommodation. Left: A superb aerial view of the River Ouse meandering alongside a busy Naburn Marina.

Half a century of personal attention

In 1947 Mr Samuel Brearley decided to leave his job in town planning to set up a company of his own. He took premises in Monkgate (which are now the premises of the firm's accountants, Garbutt and Elliott) and, in the early days, offered a civil engineering service. Since he owned a quarry, he also sold lime to farmers. Soon he was specialising in selling and laying tarmacadam. The tar was a by-product of the coal/coke industry which is not now available. It has been replaced with bituminous macadam which is made with bitumen oils.

A simple difficulty at this period was communications between office and site which could be 50 miles away and five miles from the nearest village. Two-way radios in vans and mobile phones for staff have since solved this problem.

The company stayed for twelve years in Monkgate before moving to The Ropewalk, Hallfield Road in York. The late Samuel Brearley was the company Chairman, his wife and his daughter Anne are

Directors and the present Chairman and Managing Director is his son in law Brian. Mr Brearley served on York City Council for many years, held the offices of Sheriff in 1965-1966 and Lord Mayor in 1978-1979.

The firm's markets are civil engineering projects and range from drainage and sea defences to concrete bases for industrial equipment. Their customers are local authorities, commercial and industrial clients, farmers, architects and engineers. Most quotations start with a visit to the site, with personal attention paid at every stage. The firm rarely needs to advertise and flourishes on personal recommendation.

The size of the company has been deliberately controlled so that the management has full control of all aspects of the business. In its 50th anniversary year, the company looks forward confidently to the next half century.

Above and below: Road making nearly half a century ago where traffic queues and irate motorists were a rarity.

One potato, two potato and then lots more...

RS Cockerill (York) Limited was established in the early 1930s. Ronald Cockerill originally worked in a retail ironmongers but decided that it was time for him to branch out on his own. He had rented land at Holme on Spalding Moor to grow carrots and he soon realised that he would be able to make a living out of his hobby.

At that time, during the depression, food was a continual worry for many people and the food industry seemed to be the ideal venture. He began to trade carrots and potatoes, eventually renting premises in Fawcett Street, York to market his produce. A further move was made to Kent Street, directly opposite the cattle market.

The Second World War brought new challenges for the firm. The Ministry for Food licenced it to co-

> **"THE BUSINESS BEGAN DURING THE DEPRESSION OF THE 1930S. A TIME OF SUFFERING FOR MOST PEOPLE"**

ordinate supplies for the war effort. 'Digging For Britain' became a by-word for the whole country. Much of the produce was requisitioned for the war.

At the end of the war, Ronald Cockerill took the tenancy of a farm near Stamford Bridge. This was the start of the farming activities with the purchase of Providence Farm near Dunnington in 1962, where the present potato packing and storage facilities are located. After studying agriculture at university Ronald's son, Martin Cockerill joined the company in 1967. The company has been under his leadership since the tragic death of Ronald Cockerill in a car accident in 1974.

The firm relocated their offices from Kent Street in 1970 to Hull Road when the cattle market moved to the York Livestock Centre at Murton. In 1997 the Hull Road site was sold for a large retail development and it is planned to build new offices adjacent to the packhouse at Dunnington. These will provide modern facilities to cater for the needs of the company for the foreseeable future.

Although now focused entirely on the potato market, the firm has, in the past, been involved with other activities.

Agrochemical distribution was developed in the late 1970s and for a while the firm used helicopters to spray pesticides. This business was sold in 1988 for both commercial and environmental reasons.

The company supplies potatoes to the wholesale market, multiple retailers, potato processors and cash & carry warehouses and the customer base is continually expanded to cater for the wide variety of potatoes grown in the area. Although there have been many changes over the sixty years that the firm has traded the tradition remains - to exceed both their supplier's and customer's expectations.

Above: A 1970s picture of a visiting party of growers with the late Len Catterick, RS Cockerill's manager greeting Robin Dant of Tudor Crisps (now Walkers).
Left: The offices at Kent Street behind the lorry at the top of the picture in the late 1950s.
Below: Two RS Cockerill lorries delivering potatoes to the Tudor Crisps factory at Peterlee in the mid 1970s.

York Autolectrics - servicing the needs of an ever changing market

The automobile electrical trade began its development in this country just before the First World War. When mass production methods copied from America got under way the British motor manufacturers started to fit dynamos, starters and electric lighting from about 1922. Lucas, CAV and Rotax were the three main producers of this equipment, who amalgamated in 1927. The year before Mr C.T. Marks had become an apprentice at Rotax in Taunton. When qualified he took on his first agency for these suppliers in Southport.

Piccadilly. This "Active Service Garage" had been vacated by the Airspeed Aircraft Company with which the novelist Nevil Shute was associated.

After only two months trading they purchased Scarborough Ignition Co., subsequently run by Bill Bower, a director of the company. In July 1937 a further branch was set up in Bridlington by Fred Milner, one of the original employees from York. At this stage the company still specialised in servicing and repairing autoelectric equipment such as magnetos, starters, dynamos, batteries and lights. In 1950 a diesel fuel injection repair shop was opened, initially for commercial vehicles and tractors, but more recently for cars as well. This expansion meant new premises were needed. They were acquired in Lead Mill Lane and opened in 1953. These premises were subject to a compulsory purchase order in 1967. A specially designed and spacious building was put up, giving ample room to handle the largest commercial vehicles in its garage. This proved invaluable, when the Ministry of Transport approved the company for fitting and testing tachographs.

In 1934 he was invited to develop a Lucas agency in York. With £250 of his own money and £140 from Mr T. Leedham of Leedhams Garage, they formed York Autolectrics Ltd. which began operating from part of the York Corporation bus depot in

Top: The founder Mr C. T. Marks (pictured left) outside Southport Electrical Services in 1933, one year before his move to York. *Above:* The exterior of York Autolectrics on Lead Mill Lane. *Right:* The diesel pump repair shop in Layerthorpe, 1967.

A further company was formed in 1960 called Electrical Rewinding Services (York) Ltd. This company specialises in the rewinding of burnt out mains electric motors. A highly skilled, and very specialised job essential for keeping farms and factories running smoothly.

Mr "C.T." Marks was succeeded by his son, Tim Marks in 1973, so that it still remains an old established family company which no longer has any connection with Leedhams.

In 1986 Bridlington Autolectrics was moved to Beverley so that servicing could be offered to customers in the Hull area. A change of place meant a change of name, and it was decided that the whole

group should use the trading title of Yortec. At that time the present managing director, Tim Marks said "The market today is very challenging and changes occur very rapidly indeed. We have made a lot of changes to ensure that our customers get the best possible service. By changing our name we are portraying an up-to-date company with a lot of experience and capable of meeting all the challenges of the future."

Top: Mr Jack Cummings, autoelectrician rewiring a customer's vehicle. Left: Arthur Edwards, regional manager for Joseph Lucas Ltd, presenting £5.00 to Mr Arnold Witton, Autoelectrical foreman in 1970. Also pictured are Mr Ron Hope, the Sales and Service Director, left, and Mr C. T. Marks, Managing Director, right. Below: The devastating fire at Layerthorpe in 1979.

Derwent Coachworks - specialists in body building and painting

Fred Weatherley and Bryan Jowsey, two well known people in the motor industry in Yorkshire,.founded Derwent Coachworks in 1951.

Fred had been a panel-beater and welder employed by Unwins, the main Ford dealer in York. He was almost certainly the first specialist panel-beater employed in York as the work had previously been carried out by mechanics.

Bryan was an apprentice engineer at the LNER workshops. Both were Scout masters in a very successful Scout troop until they went into the forces, Bryan flying Lancasters in the RAF and Fred in the REME. On demobilisation they chose business in the car body trade.

The partners rented land at Osbaldwick on the outskirts of York. In five weeks, with the help of one bricklayer the new premises were complete and the first customer had arrived. At first the work was mostly rebuilding MoD vehicles and the repair and painting of cars for private customers. Gradually subcontracted work was carried out for larger garages. After the first year extra

staff were employed. Both partners shared most tasks and inside two years the first commercial vehicle contract came from National Glass Works to paint the bodywork on a fleet of thirty trucks. Workshop size was doubled and the staff increased to six.

Preparation work was done outside in the yard and then the vehicles were brush painted by Bryan. Up to this time most cars were black but during the fifties other colours gained popularity and to meet this demand a highly skilled specialist colour matching facility was developed which increased demand.

In the early 1960s Bryan and Fred purchased land near the city centre and a new, larger workshop and offices were built and the

repair department expanded. Coachbuilding was extended to build many fleets for Rowntree, Esso, BRS and many others. At first most vehicles had timber frames.

Top Left: Fred Weatherley in uniform during the War.
Top right: Bryan Jowsey in his RAF uniform.
Above and left: Two examples of the trucks built for national fleets like Esso during the 1960s and the Centenary celebration trucks for Boyes in the early 1980s.

In 1963 they took over the well established joinery company Messrs Wm. Bellerby Ltd which was expanded to take on the building of schools,

They also fitted vehicles with such equipment as tail lifts, heaters and generators. Even so, car repair and painting still accounted for 50% of the turnover.

The partnership is thriving with many new ventures being developed.

Top: *The production line of tipper trucks for North Eastern Electric.*
Inset: *A cattle truck fitted out in the early 1970s.*
Left: *A travelling exhibition unit for the TSB.*
Below: *A car in the workshop for accident repair and repainting, still a major part of the business today.*

housing and public works for local authorities. This business was sold in the 1970s as the demand for general woodworking declined. From this time aluminium became the main structural material and reinforced plastics were becoming important.

From the late seventies coachbuilding work diversified and the firm began producing ambulances, minibuses and refrigerated and tipping vehicles.

Turnbulls of York - looking after the discerning motorist for almost half a century

Turnbulls, the successful Mazda dealership located along Layerthorpe Road in York is approaching the milestone of half a century in business. The company was established in March 1952 by Robert Turnbull.

The founder was no stranger to enterprise and had already experienced success in the motor industry. From a very modest start Robert Turnbull built up his capital with a car repair business in his home town of Harrogate.
Close attention to the needs of his customers, and a natural gift

Robert Turnbull
Founded the business in the early 1950s

Peter Turnbull
joined his father in 1958

Martyn Turnbull
and his brother
Paul Turnbull
joined their father in the mid 1980s

with all things mechanical resulted in the growth of the business and this enabled Robert to extend the scope of his activities into petrol retailing.

The early days in York
After a long search for a suitable location the site of a run-down filling station and garage in York was identified and acquired. Much modernisation was required - old-fashioned petrol pumps which swung across the pavement were still in use when Robert Turnbull took over! With remarkable self-belief and faith in his own ability, Robert set about the task of modernising and rebuilding the site to meet the

needs of the increasingly discerning 1950s motorist.

Servicing cars and selling petrol from Holgate Bridge Filling Station continued for a decade until the business was sold in 1962. During the following five years Robert operated from a busy petrol station located at Monkbridge, York, selling *Cleveland* fuel. The Cleveland organisation was later bought out by the mighty 'Esso' corporation.

Peter Turnbull, Robert's son, had joined his father in the family business in 1958 and began selling cars to a growing band of eager customers by 1961.

The move to Layerthorpe Road
Next came the move to the present site, 17-27 Layerthorpe Road, in 1967 and a change in the trading name to 'R & P Turnbull' reflecting Peter Turnbull's increasing contribution to the running of the business.

Expansion characterised the following years and the development of the business. A crucial milestone in the history of the company was passed when it secured the franchise for Mazda cars. Mazda U.K. Ltd. are known to be very demanding of the individual dealers which make up their network, and Turnbulls appointment in the York area was one of their proudest moments.

One of the signs of a successful business is undoubtedly the level of repeat business it manages to achieve. This is yet another source of pride at Turnbulls of York as they have individual customers

Left: Turnbulls state-of-the-art premises on Layerthorpe Road.

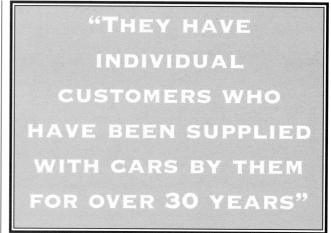

who have been supplied with cars by them for over 30 years. Most of these highly satisfied customers are private individuals and the principals of many of the small businesses which thrive in York and the surrounding district. There are exceptions to this - and a significant proportion of the business is secured from other parts of the U.K. - and the occasional export order, including one from Pakistan!

Further expansion
It has been a challenge for the premises at Layerthorpe Road to cope with the expansion of the business over the years. Land has been acquired at the side and rear of the original site to allow for the growth and a superbly equipped workshop complete with state-of-the-art technology sits at the hub of the Turnbull Mazda operation. An ever growing band of delighted customers is assured by the after-sales expertise of Martyn and Paul Turnbull, grandsons of the founder, who have been involved in the business since the mid-1980s.

The motor trade is more competitive than ever as it enters the dawn of a new millennium, and many of the smaller independent motor dealerships have been swallowed up by the more impersonal national chains.

Personal service and quality cars
Personal service and attention to detail are just two of the formidable weapons in the Turnbull armoury. These, combined with the quality and renowned reliability of the Mazda cars which are sold by the company will ensure that Turnbulls Mazda will continue to look after the interests of its customers well into the next century. A point illustrated by one valued client who visited the dealership after a long absence and explained: "I have kept my present car far too long because it has been so reliable."

The Household Cavalry entering the city through Micklegate Bar on June 28th 1971.

A 1955 photograph showing the city walls and immaculate embankment.